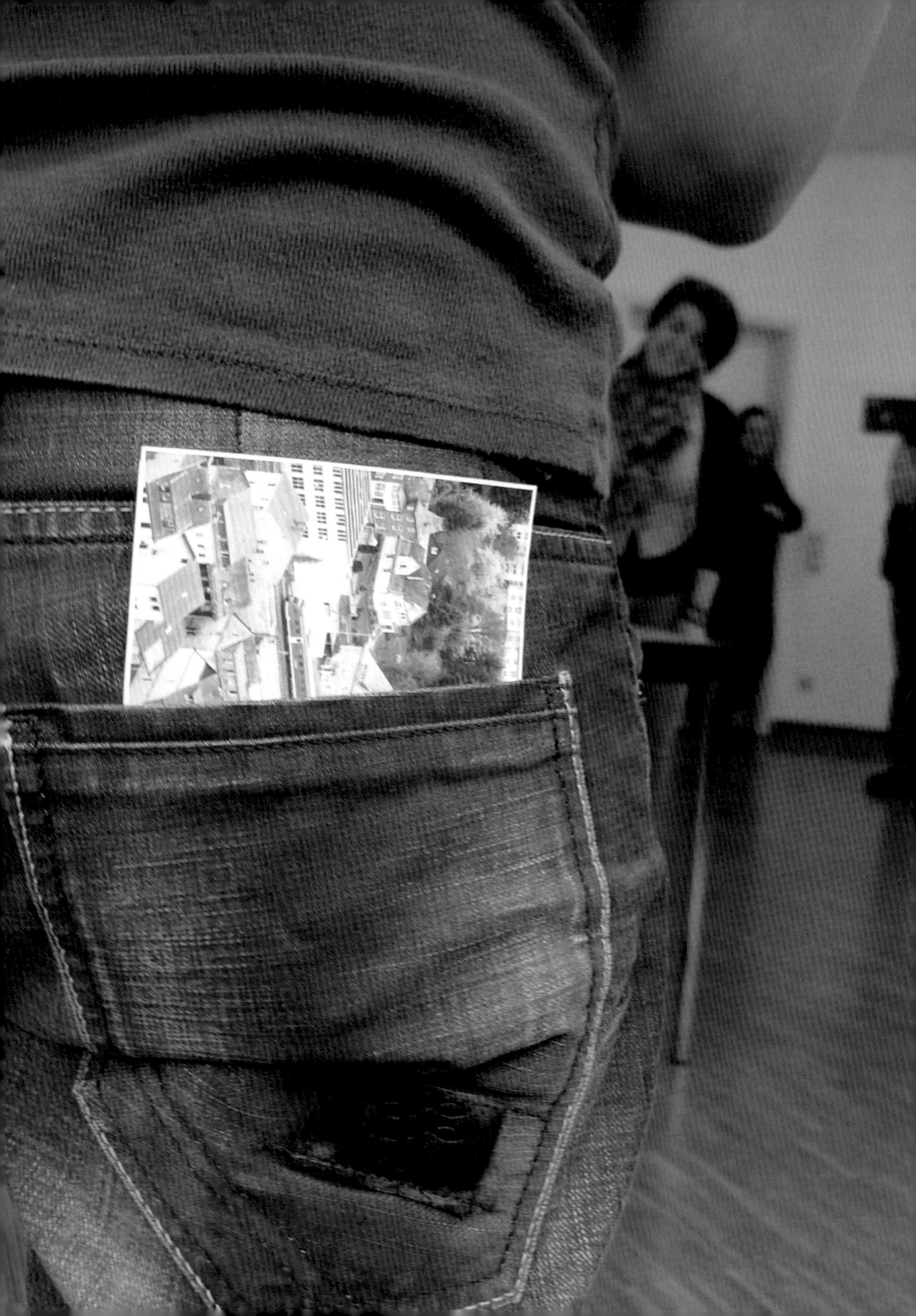

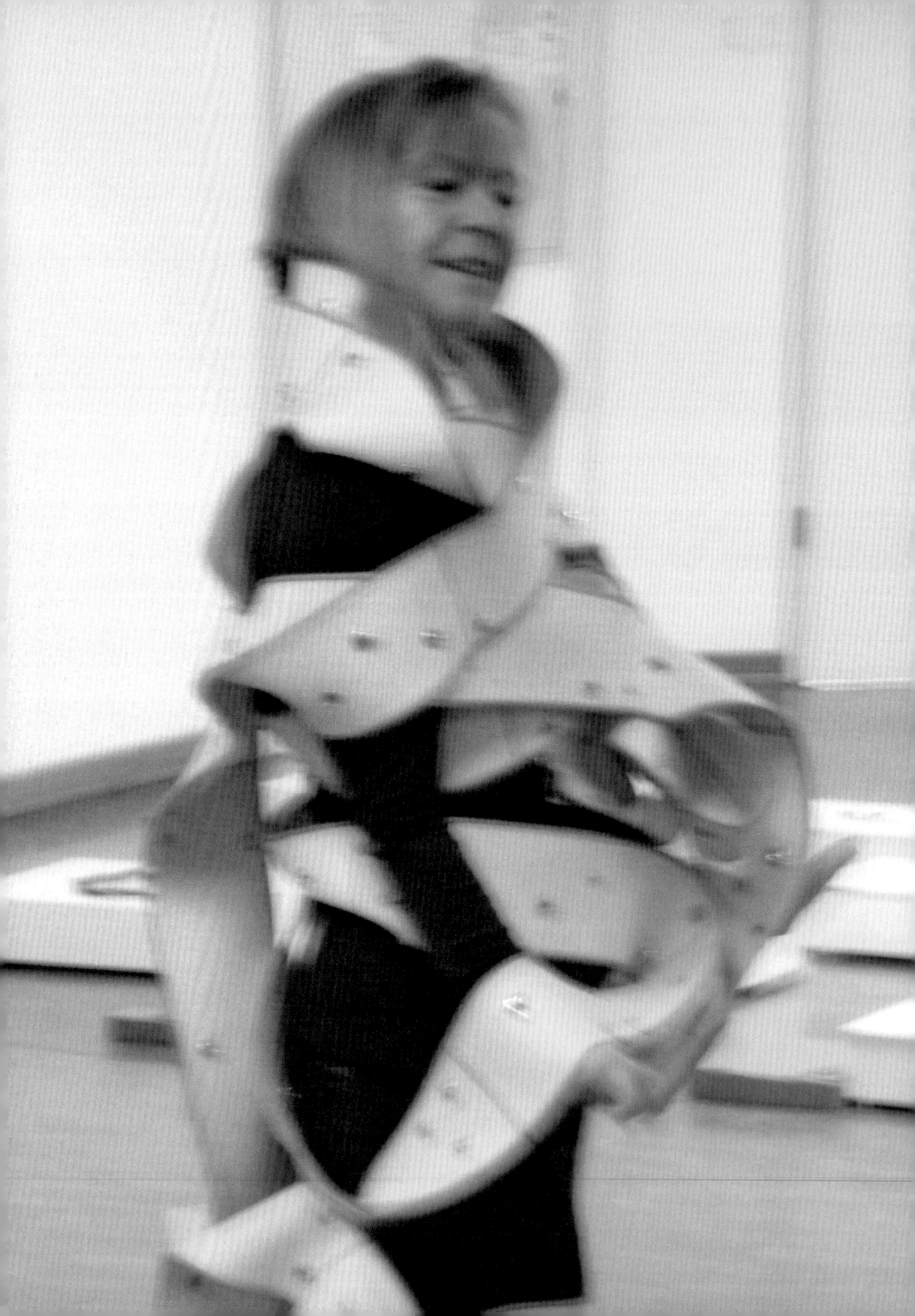

nsaio⁶
Neuer Schmuck aus Idar-Oberstein
New Jewellery from Idar-Oberstein

arnoldsche ART PUBLISHERS

Inhalt | content

20 Neuer Schmuck aus Idar-Oberstein
New Jewellery from Idar-Oberstein
Elisabeth Dühr

22 Einleitung | Introduction
Ute Eitzenhöfer, Theo Smeets

28 Über Edelsteine, Steine und Werte
On Gemstones, Stones and Values
Ute Eitzenhöfer

34 Edelsteine im Schmuck: zwischen Bling-Bling und Kunst
Gemstones in Jewellery: between Bling and Art
Wilhelm Lindemann

48 Schmuck im Kontext
Jewellery in Context
Marjan Unger

61 reMake

62 Schmuck im Museum
Jewellery in a Museum
Julia Wild

105 Stein – Schmuck – Kunst 2006–2016
Stone – Jewellery – Art 2006–2016

329 Zum Studium | On the Study

330 Notizen zur künstlerischen Grundlehre
Notes on Teaching the Basics of Art
Eva-Maria Kollischan

336 Zur Philosophie der Fachrichtung
On Department Philosophy
Theo Smeets

345 Autorenbiografien | Authors' Biographies

347 Team | Staff

348 Register | Index

350 Impressum | Imprint

Neuer Schmuck aus Idar-Oberstein

Die Hochschule zu Gast im Stadtmuseum Simeonstift Trier

Ein Museum ist ein Ort der Erinnerung. Die Objekte, die dort für die Nachwelt bewahrt werden, erhalten ihre Bedeutung nicht nur durch ihre kostbare Materialität, historische Einzigartigkeit und vollendete Kunstfertigkeit, sondern vor allem durch die Geschichten, die sie erzählen. Persönliche Erlebnisse und schicksalhafte Ereignisse fließen in den Kunstwerken und Relikten zu einem Bild der Vergangenheit zusammen und machen sie zu unersetzlichen Kleinoden, die die Zeit hinterlassen hat.

Ähnlich verhält es sich mit Schmuck. Es sind nicht alleine die Qualität des Werkstoffs und die handwerkliche Finesse, die seinen Wert ausmachen. Vielmehr sind es die narrativen Geheimnisse, die er in sich birgt. Als persönliches Andenken an seine Trägerinnen und Träger und seine Zeit hat er einen ideellen Wert, der mit Gold nicht aufzuwiegen ist.

Die Studierenden haben diese beiden Bereiche auf intelligente, kreative und poetische Weise zusammengeführt. Die Fachrichtung Edelstein und Schmuck am Campus Idar-Oberstein der Hochschule Trier präsentiert im Rahmen dieser Ausstellung nicht nur außergewöhnliche Arbeiten aus den eigenen Ateliers. Ausgehend von der kulturhistorischen Sammlung des Stadtmuseums sind neue Werke entstanden, die zentrale Themen der Trierer Stadtgeschichte aus einem zeitgenössischen Blickwinkel betrachten. Mit historischem Bewusstsein und künstlerischem Gespür wurden die Geschichten ausgewählter Museumsstücke aufgearbeitet und weitererzählt. Durch das Medium Schmuck wurde ihnen das persönlich-intime Moment zurückgegeben, das diese Gegenstände einst mit dem Schicksal ihres Besitzers verbunden hat. Ich freue mich, dass der Erinnerungsschatz unseres Museums auf diese Weise bereichert wird.

Elisabeth Dühr
Stadtmuseum Simeonstift Trier
Direktorin

New Jewellery from Idar-Oberstein

The Trier University of Applied Sciences, a guest at the City Museum Simeonstift Trier

A museum is a place of remembrance. The objects that are conserved there for posterity are significant not only because of their valuable materiality, historical uniqueness or accomplished craftsmanship but, above all, because of the stories that they tell. Personal experiences and fateful events merge through works of art and relics into an image of the past and transform them into irreplaceable treasures that time left behind.

It is similar for jewellery. It is not just the quality of the raw materials or the hand-crafted finesse which determine the value of a piece of jewellery but rather the narrative secrets they hold. As a personal keepsake of its wearer and its era, it has a sentimental value that cannot be measured in terms of money.

The students have intelligently, creatively and poetically united these two areas. The Department of Gemstones and Jewellery at the Idar-Oberstein campus of the Trier University of Applied Sciences, does not only present exceptional work from their own studio in this exhibition. Based upon the culturally historical collection of the Stadtmuseum, new pieces have also been created which examine central themes of the history of Trier from a contemporary perspective. The stories of selected museum exhibits have been reclaimed and continued with historical awareness and artistic flair. The medium of jewellery has restored a personally intimate moment for them which once connected these items to the fate of their owners. I am delighted that the treasure of memories of our museum has been enriched in such a way.

Elisabeth Dühr
City Museum Simeonstift Trier
Director

Einleitung
Ute Eitzenhöfer und Theo Smeets

nsaio, „neuer Schmuck aus Idar-Oberstein", steht seit nunmehr 15 Jahren für die Präsentation von Arbeiten der Studierenden der Hochschule Trier in Idar-Oberstein. Es ist eine Art verbindende Klammer für höchst unterschiedliche Arbeiten, denn wir legen besonderen Wert darauf, Individualität und persönliche Handschrift in einer möglichst großen Brandbreite zu fördern. So ist es nicht verwunderlich, dass es vorrangiges Ziel der Fachrichtung Edelstein und Schmuck ist, die Studierenden auf dem Weg zu frei agierenden, aber kritischen Menschen und vor allem zu eigenständigen Künstlerinnen und Künstlern mit einer einzigartigen Identität zu begleiten.

Das vorliegende Buch dokumentiert Arbeiten der Studierenden seit 2006 und gibt somit auch einen Einblick in die Entwicklung der Fachrichtung.

Wie der Standort Idar-Oberstein vermuten lässt, geht es im Studium des Bachelor und Master of Fine Arts neben der freien künstlerischen Arbeit, dem Thema Schmuck und Schmücken auch – und oft vor allem – um Edelsteine. Sie müssen zwar nicht in jeder Arbeit vorhanden sein, doch eine Haltung zum Material soll entwickelt werden. Das Studium in einem Edelsteinzentrum setzt diese Auseinandersetzung voraus.

Eine Publikation stellt auch immer eine Momentaufnahme in einem Prozess dar. So ist dieses Buch anlässlich der gleichnamigen Ausstellung nsaio[6] im Trierer Stadtmuseum Simeonstift entstanden. Es ist für die hier vorgestellten jungen Künstlerinnen und Künstler von sehr großem Wert, nicht nur in einer Publikation, sondern auch bei einer Ausstellung an einem prominenten und kulturträchtigen Ort – direkt neben der weltberühmten Porta Nigra – vertreten zu sein. Eine solche Ausstellung ist, noch während des Studiums und darüber hinaus, ein Ansporn, den nicht ganz leichten Weg in der Welt des Schmucks weiterzugehen und sich nicht beirren zu lassen, sich nicht anzupassen und die Entwürfe auf rein ökonomische Gesichtspunkte zu reduzieren. Vielmehr ist es unbedingt notwendig, beharrlich dem gewählten Weg zu folgen, der begonnenen Entwicklung Zeit zum Reifen zu gönnen und so die gesellschaftliche Aufgabe der Angewandten Kunst als dauerhaftes, gesellschaftsbezogenes Statement zu begreifen.

Das Studienangebot der Hochschule in Idar-Oberstein ist weltweit einmalig – Edelstein- und Schmuckgestaltung können hier auf Bachelor- und Masterniveau studiert werden. Dieses Angebot zieht erfreulicherweise besonders motivierte und zielstrebige Bewerberinnen und Bewerber an, denn insbesondere die Arbeit mit Edelsteinen ist sehr komplex, verlangt Fingerspitzengefühl,

Introduction
Ute Eitzenhöfer and Theo Smeets

nsaio, "neuer Schmuck aus Idar-Oberstein" [New Jewellery from Idar-Oberstein] has stood for fifteen years now for the presentation of student work at the Hochschule Trier in Idar-Oberstein. It is a sort of all-encompassing parenthesis linking highly diverse works because we attach particular importance to promoting individuality and personal signatures within a range that is as broad as possible. Unsurprisingly, therefore, the Department of Gemstones and Jewellery gives priority to accompanying students on their way to acting as free yet critical agents and, most importantly, developing into independent artists, each with their own distinctive identity.

The present book documents student work since 2006, thus providing insight into the way the department has evolved.

As its location in Idar-Oberstein suggests, the course of study leading to bachelor and master of fine arts degrees, along with independent art work, is about the subject of jewellery and adornment – and, often in the first instance, gemstones. They need not be present in every work, yet an attitude to the material is to be developed. Studying at a gemstone centre is premised on this investigation and its ramifications.

Also a publication invariably represents a freeze-frame shot in an ongoing process. Thus this book has been created to accompany the exhibition of the same name, nsaio[6], at the City Museum Simeonstift in Trier. It is of great importance to the young artists introduced here to be represented not only in a publication but also at an exhibition organised in a place that is so distinguished and steeped in culture – abutting the world-famous Porta Nigra. An exhibition of this kind and on this scale provides students with an incentive, while they are still studying and afterwards, to continue on their way in the world of jewellery, which is not the easiest path to take, and to not let themselves be led astray, become conformists or reduce design to purely economic considerations. On the contrary, it is absolutely necessary for them to continue tenaciously on the path they have chosen, to give themselves time for the development they have embarked on to mature and thus define the social mission of the exponents of the applied arts as a lasting statement with reference to society.

The curriculum offered by the university of applied sciences in Idar-Oberstein is unique worldwide – gemstone and jewellery design can be studied here at bachelor and master degree level. Fortunately, the range of courses offered attracts particularly motivated and focused applicants because working with gem-

sehr viel Geduld und oft Durchsetzungsvermögen sowie einen umfassenden Gestaltungswillen.

Die momentan etwa 50 Studierenden in der Fachrichtung Edelstein und Schmuck stammen aus fast 20 verschiedenen Ländern, sodass an unserem Hochschulstandort alle Studierenden und Lehrenden ständig mit den verschiedensten Meinungen und kulturellen, politischen, sozialen und künstlerischen Standpunkten umgeben sind. Eine Vielfalt, die es ermöglicht, Dinge und Verhaltensweisen aus einer völlig anderen, oft auch völlig neuen Perspektive zu sehen. Schon durch das Zusammenkommen der Studierenden aus aller Welt wird eines der wichtigsten Gestaltungsprinzipien, die Abschaffung von Grenzen, ein selbstverständlicher Teil des Alltags.

Nach der Gründung der Fachrichtung 1986 wurde die Aufbauphase von einem Team begeisterter ehemaliger Kollegen unter der Ägide der Professoren Udo Ackermann und Rolf Müller getragen. Um den Jahrtausendwechsel fand die Stabweitergabe statt. Durch sie wurde die vom Gründungsteam angedachte künstlerische Ausrichtung der Abteilung weiter ausgebaut und mündete schließlich im momentanen Studienangebot im Bereich Fine Arts. Seit 2003 – als für kurze Zeit die Existenz der Fachrichtung aus Kostengründen in Frage gestellt wurde – hat es am Standort Idar-Oberstein wesentliche Entwicklungen gegeben. Die Hochschule hat, neben der Aktualisierung der Lehrinhalte und der Umstellung auf Bachelor- und Masterstudienangebote, auch für die Edelsteinregion Idar-Oberstein eine entscheidende Rolle beim Aufbau eines international beachteten Kulturprogramms im Bereich Edelsteine und Schmuck übernommen. Gemeinsam mit der Stadt Idar-Oberstein und dem Kreis Birkenfeld wurde ein vielschichtiges Konzept zum kulturellen Aufbau und zur Erweiterung des Standortes entwickelt und umgesetzt. Eine besondere Rolle kommt dabei Wilhelm Lindemann zu – ihm gilt unser großer und besonderer Dank!

Im Rahmen des Kulturprogramms finden an der Hochschule seit 2005 die Symposien „SchmuckDenken" statt. Die gleichnamige Publikation zur Symposienreihe gehört mittlerweile zur Standardliteratur an vielen Hochschulen weltweit.

Eine weitere Maßnahme für die Standortsicherung ist die von Wilhelm Lindemann initiierte und von der Stadt Idar-Oberstein mitgetragene Umwandlung der Bengelfabrik in ein Kulturdenkmal mit Ausstellungsraum für zeitgenössischen Schmuck. Dort ist eine mittlerweile vielbeachtete Bühne für die internationale Schmuckkunstszene entstanden: unter der Überschrift „Idar-Oberstein schmückt sich" werden unter künstlerischer Leitung der Hochschule in der Villa Bengel jährlich etwa zehn Ausstellungen von international renommierten Schmuckkünstlerinnen und -künstlern veranstaltet.

stones is especially complex, requires sure instincts, a great deal of patience and often assertiveness as well as an all-encompassing desire to design.

There are currently some fifty students in the Department of Gemstones and Jewellery. They come from nearly twenty different countries with the result that all students and instructors at our university of applied sciences are always surrounded with a wide variety of opinions and cultural, political, social and artistic viewpoints. This diversity makes it possible to see things and behaviour patterns from entirely different angles and to develop often entirely new perspectives on them. Students gathering in one place from all over the world is in itself one of the most important design principles; the elimination of boundaries is part of everyday life that is taken for granted.

After the department was established in 1986, the start-up phase was supported by a team of enthusiastic former colleagues headed by Professors Udo Ackermann and Rolf Müller. At the turn of the millennium the baton changed hands. This change in leadership enabled the artistic orientation of the department as planned by the founder team to be consolidated and has ultimately led to the present fine arts curriculum. Since 2003 – when there was briefly a question mark over the survival of the department for financial reasons – crucial developments have taken place in Idar-Oberstein. Apart from updating curricula and switching to courses of study leading to bachelor's and master's degrees, the university of applied sciences has played a vital role in building up an internationally acclaimed cultural programme in the field of gemstones and jewellery. Together with the city of Idar-Oberstein and the district of Birkenfeld, a multilayered concept for cultural development and for the enlargement of the department has been thought out and realised. Wilhelm Lindemann has played a leading role in this – to him we are grateful indeed and owe our special thanks!

Since 2005 the 'SchmuckDenken' [ThinkingJewellery] symposia have been held at the university of applied sciences under the aegis of the cultural programme. The publication accompanying the symposia by now belongs to the standard reference works in many a university library across the world.

Initiated by Wilhelm Lindemann and co-sponsored by the city of Idar-Oberstein, another measure that has consolidated the department's reputation is the transformation of the Bengel factory into a cultural monument with an exhibition space for contemporary jewellery. The former Bengel factory has become an acclaimed stage for the international jewellery scene: under the heading "Idar-Oberstein schmückt sich" [Idar-Oberstein Adorns Itself], some ten exhibitions a year of the work of internationally renowned artists in jewellery are organised at Villa Bengel with the university of applied sciences as curator.

Nicht zuletzt gibt es seit zehn Jahren das Artist-in-Residence-Programm. Etwa sechs Monate im Jahr sind Schmuckkünstlerinnen und -künstler vor Ort und entdecken die Möglichkeiten der omnipräsenten Edelsteine sowie der alten Ketten- und Schmuckmanufaktur Jakob Bengel. Gleichzeitig bildet dieses Programm ein wichtiges Glied bei der studentischen Orientierung hinsichtlich der Berufspraxis.

Einen möglichst fruchtbaren Nährboden für die künstlerische Entwicklung aller Studierenden in Idar-Oberstein zu schaffen, ist unsere Aufgabe. Deren Individualität als gleichberechtigte Möglichkeiten von Identität nebeneinander zu stellen, ist ein wesentliches Anliegen des Studiums, der Ausstellung nsaio[6] im Trierer Stadtmuseum Simeonstift und dieses Katalogs. Dieses Anliegen zu realisieren, ist nur möglich, indem wir jeden Tag eine gute und gemeinschaftliche Teamarbeit anstreben, um so die Studierenden in ihren vielfältigen Bedürfnissen möglichst individuell zu betreuen. Wir bedanken uns daher an dieser Stelle nicht nur bei den Studierenden für alle wundervollen Arbeiten, die sie erschaffen haben und die hier vorgestellt werden können, sondern auch bei unseren Mitarbeiterinnen und Mitarbeitern, die ihre Aufgabe mit großem Engagement angehen und so wesentlich zum Erfolg unserer Studierenden, Absolventinnen und Absolventen beitragen.

Es gilt unser herzlicher Dank dem Stadtmuseum Simeonstift für die Möglichkeit, junge Arbeiten so prominent und in solch großem Umfang zu präsentieren. Auch das in diesem Buch enthaltene Projekt „reMake", in dem Studierende mit ihren Arbeiten auf Sammlungsstücke des Museums reagieren, ist ein gutes Beispiel für eine sinnvolle, praxisnahe und dennoch künstlerisch anspruchsvolle Kooperation zwischen dem Museum Simeonstift und der Hochschule in Idar-Oberstein.

Wir wünschen Ihnen viel Spaß, erstaunliche Entdeckungen und schöne Überraschungen bei der Lektüre von nsaio[6].

Last but not least, the university of applied sciences has had an artist-in-residence programme for ten years. For about six months every year artists in jewellery are in Idar-Oberstein to discover the possibilities of the omnipresent gemstones as well as the old Jakob Bengel chain and jewellery factory. At the same time this programme represents an important link in helping students to choose their professional orientation.

Our task is to create as fertile soil as possible for all students to develop their creativity in Idar-Oberstein. A key concern of their course of study, the nsaio[6] exhibition at the City Museum Simeonstift in Trier and this catalogue is to present their individuality as the possibilities of identity on an equal footing. Realising this concern is only possible if we strive each day for good, communal teamwork in order to mentor students with all their diverse needs as individually as possible. Hence we thank at this juncture not only our students for all the wonderful works they have created that are to be presented here but also our staff, who have approached their task with unswerving commitment, thus contributing crucially to the success of our students and graduates.

We should like to express our heartfelt thanks to the City Museum Simeonstift for enabling us to present the works of young artists in such a distinguished context and on such a grand scale. The re*Make* project, in which students react to pieces in the museum collection with works of their own, is another good example of the meaningful, practical yet aesthetically sophisticated cooperation between the Museum Simeonstift and the university of applied sciences in Idar-Oberstein.

We wish you a lot of fun, astonishing discoveries, and beautiful surprises while reading nsaio[6].

Über Edelsteine, Steine und Werte
Ute Eitzenhöfer

Über Edelsteine
Wir stellen Ihnen mit dem Buch nsaio[6] Arbeiten vor, die sich sowohl mit dem Thema Edelstein als auch mit den Themen Schmuck und Schmücken auseinandersetzen.

Wenn Edelstein in einem Schmuckstück verwendet werden soll, so ist es zuerst einmal notwendig zu klären, was das für ein Material ist, das verwendet werden soll. Die Auseinandersetzung mit Edelsteinen lässt sich dabei nicht an der bloßen Verwendung des eigentlichen Materials festmachen. Vielmehr geht es zunächst darum, sich mit ihren Eigenschaften und mit den gesellschaftlich zugeschriebenen Attributen vertraut zu machen, um dann zu hinterfragen, wie diese in die künstlerische Arbeit einbezogen werden können.

In der heutigen Zeit mit Edelsteinen zu arbeiten, stellt geradezu einen Antagonismus dar. Denn man darf Eines ganz bestimmt nicht erwarten, wenn man damit arbeitet: dass es schnell geht. In Zeiten, in denen eine Nachricht in Sekunden um die ganze Welt geht, werden die Studierenden mit etwas konfrontiert, was der bisherigen Erlebniswelt vieler nicht entspricht. Edelsteine fordern in ihrer Bearbeitung einiges an Geduld und Muße. Sie sind hart, sie widersetzen sich, sie lassen sich nur mit Mühe bearbeiten, sie springen, wenn ein Riss übersehen wird. Und wenn sie einmal gesprungen sind, dann gibt es weder die Möglichkeit zu kitten, noch einfach ein neues Stück zu nehmen und von vorn zu beginnen. Denn sie sind Naturprodukte – und somit einzigartig.

Solch ein Material braucht Zeit. Künstlerische Arbeit braucht Zeit. Und gerade jetzt, in einer Welt, in der alles berechnet wird, in der es den Anschein hat, alles sei auf Zahlen reduzierbar, sind Räume wichtig, in denen das Experiment erlaubt sein darf. Räume, in denen es erlaubt ist, nur wahrnehmen zu dürfen, ohne bewerten zu müssen. Räume, in denen Ambivalenzen existieren dürfen und in denen gelernt werden kann, mit diesen Ambivalenzen umzugehen, ohne sich fortwährend für das Eine oder Andere entscheiden zu müssen. Ein gutes künstlerisches Ergebnis entsteht nicht dadurch, dass ein ganzer Prozess durchgetaktet ist. Ein gutes Ergebnis entsteht aus fundierter Auseinandersetzung mit dem Thema und seiner rigoros freien Bearbeitung.

Über Steine
Wie kann das uralte Material Stein in die heutige Zeit eingeordnet werden? Was bewirkt es, auf einen Stein zu treffen, der so schön ist, dass alles, was hinzugefügt wird, im Grunde genommen nicht notwendig ist? Hier muss es erlaubt

On Gemstones, Stones and Values

Ute Eitzenhöfer

On gemstones

In the book nsaio[6], we are introducing you to works that deal with the subject of gemstones as well as the subjects of jewellery and personal adornment.

If gemstones are to be used in a piece of jewellery, it is first of all necessary to clarify what kind of material is to be used. Investigating gemstones cannot be linked with the mere use of what is actually the material. Rather, what is at stake is, first of all, familiarising oneself with the properties and the attributes society imputes to gemstones in order to question how those properties and attributes may be incorporated in a work of art.

Working with gemstones nowadays represents what is really a contradiction in terms. After all, there is one thing that cannot be expected of anyone working with them: that it will be quick work. In an age in which a news item can speed round the world in seconds, students are being confronted with something that does not tally with the world as many of them have experienced it. Working gemstones exacts quite a bit of patience and leisure. They are hard, they are intractable, working them is a laborious process and they shatter if a crack has escaped notice. And once they have shattered, there is no possibility of cementing them together again or simply of taking a fresh piece and starting over again from the beginning. For they are products of nature – hence each is unique.

A material of this kind needs time. Working as an artist takes time. And nowadays in a world in which everything is calculated, in which everything seems to have been reduced to numbers, having spaces in which experimentation is permitted is important. Spaces in which one is permitted simply to perceive without having to evaluate. Spaces in which ambivalences may exist and in which one can learn how to deal with those ambivalences without having to opt constantly for one thing or another. A good artistic outcome does not result from a process that has been timed throughout. A good outcome results from knowledgeable investigation of the subject and working it up in rigorously championed freedom.

On stones

How can a material as primordial as stone be classified in today's world? What is the impact made by encountering a stone so beautiful that everything that can be added to it is basically extraneous? Proclaiming that beauty alone may not always suffice must be permitted at this stage. Or that it is simply necessary

sein kundzutun, dass Schönheit allein vielleicht nicht immer reicht. Oder dass es notwendig ist, der Schönheit einfach noch mehr Schönheit hinzuzufügen. Natürlich kann die Frage gestellt werden, wie Schönheit überhaupt definiert ist. Aber: Wie weit hilft diese Frage?

Über Werte
Was betrachten wir als wertvoll? Was ist ein Wert und warum ist etwas wertvoll?

Was wir von außen sehen, zeigt nur einen Teil der Geschichte. Dinge können nie von allen Seiten gleichzeitig betrachtet werden. Eine andere Seite zu betrachten, kann enttäuschen, weil ich nur das sehe, was ich erwartet habe – oder sie kann neue Möglichkeiten bieten. Denn anders zu schauen eröffnet andere Perspektiven. Aber ist es überhaupt notwendig, den Dingen auf den Grund zu gehen? Oder: Ist es notwendig, seine Zeit damit zu verschwenden, unnötige Dinge zu tun? Welchen Nutzen bringt das? Was ist unumgänglich, was nicht? Welchen Nutzen hat es, irgendwo einfach nur herum zu laufen? Welchen Nutzen hat es, Steine anzuschauen anstatt sie zu schleifen?

Diese Fragen haben nicht nur allein mit künstlerischer Arbeit und ihren Bezügen zu tun. Sie haben auch mit der Frage zu tun: Wie lebe ich in dieser Welt und in dieser Gesellschaft und inwiefern ist es möglich, sie zu beeinflussen?

Über Ewigkeit
Wilhelm Lindemann, ehemals Kulturbeauftragter der Stadt Idar-Oberstein, sieht die Edelsteine als ein Zeichen für Ewigkeit in einer Plastikwelt. Steine und Edelsteine zählten schon immer zu den begehrtesten Werkstoffen. Und sie sind als Symbol für die Ewigkeit noch sehr viel geeigneter als Gold. Ein Stein kann nicht wieder eingeschmolzen und weiterverwendet werden wie Edelmetall. Der Schliff, den jemand einem Stein gibt, wird bleiben.

Die einzige Möglichkeit, ihn zu verändern ist, Material wegzunehmen. Wenn die ursprüngliche Form so geändert wird, wird der Stein kleiner. Jeder, der an einem Stein seine Spuren hinterlassen möchte, trägt dazu bei, dass er verschwindet. Man ist geradezu versucht zu glauben, dass Steine es einem nicht verzeihen, wenn ihre Ewigkeit zerstört werden soll.

Über Zeit
Freie Zeit – ich würde sie eher als leere Zeit bezeichnen – ist keine Zeitverschwendung. Ist Zeit – wenn Sie nicht mit Aktivitäten angefüllt ist – verlorene Zeit? Das Nichts scheint schwierig zu sein. Keine Möglichkeit verpassen. Jede Minute nutzen. Alles an Information aufnehmen, was geht. Soviel Information, bis kein Platz

to add even more beauty to something already beautiful. Of course the question of how to define beauty anyway can be raised. But how helpful is this question?

On values
What do we regard as valuable? What is a value and why is something valuable?

What we see from the outside only shows part of the story. Things can never be viewed from all sides synchronously. Looking at another side can be disappointing because I only see what I have expected to see. Or the other side can provide new possibilities. After all, looking with different eyes opens up different perspectives. But is getting to the bottom of things even necessary? Or: does one need to waste one's time on doing unnecessary things? What use is that? What is unavoidable? What isn't? What is the use of simply running around somewhere? What is the use of looking at stones instead of grinding and polishing them?

These questions do not have to do solely with working in art and related issues. They also have to do with the question, how do I live in this world and this society and to what extent is it possible to influence them?

On eternity
Wilhelm Lindemann, formerly chargé d'affaires for culture for the city of Idar-Oberstein, views precious stones as a sign of eternity in a world of plastic. Stones and gemstones have always been one of the most sought-after materials to work with. And they are far more suited to being symbols of eternity than gold is. A stone cannot be melted down and reused as a noble metal can. The cut that someone gives a stone will remain.

The only possibility of changing a stone is to take material away from it. When its original form is altered in this way, a stone becomes smaller. Anyone who wants to leave traces of himself on a stone contributes to its disappearance. One is actually tempted to believe that stones are unforgiving if their claim to eternity is destroyed.

On time
Free time – I'd tend to call it empty time – is not a waste of time. Is time – if it isn't filled with activities – lost time? Doing nothing seems difficult. Don't miss out on any possibility. Use every minute. Absorb all the information possible. So much information until there is no room for anything else. How can it be possible to reflect on what has been experienced if time and space are lost on this?

When eating, it takes time afterwards to digest what has been eaten. When one's head is stuffed with information, one needs time to lean back and

mehr für Anderes ist. Wie soll es möglich sein, Erlebtes zu reflektieren, wenn Zeit und Raum dafür verloren gehen?

Wenn man isst, braucht es danach Zeit, um zu verdauen. Wenn der Kopf voller Information ist, braucht es Zeit, um sich zurücklehnen zu können, das, was passiert ist, nochmals zu betrachten. Nochmals darüber nachzudenken, was ich gehört oder gesehen habe. Der Versuch zu klären, die Essenz zu finden oder vielleicht ganz einfach nur den Kopf leer zu machen, um Dinge mit Abstand von Neuem betrachten zu können. Eine Zeit, die notwendig sein kann, um Störendes oder Unwichtiges zu erkennen.

Über das Schmücken

Unsere Studierenden haben gewählt, Schmuck zu machen, denn sie finden darin ein Medium, mit dem es ihnen möglich ist „zu sprechen". Und ich bin sehr begeistert darüber, dass es oft ein „Verstehen" gibt, wenn jemand Schmuckstücke betrachtet oder kauft. Aber in dem Moment, in dem jemand mehr wissen will, zurück will auf die übliche Ebene der Sprache, erklärt werden soll, was das jetzt ist, erklärt werden soll, welche Idee genau dahinter steckt, erklärt werden soll, warum das jetzt berührt – bleibt immer ein Teil der Frage unbeantwortet. Denn das Reden reduziert sich oft auf die Bestätigung einer formalen Wahl. Es kann nicht in Gänze vermitteln, was das Gefühl gewählt hat. Letztendlich findet ein Rest an Kommunikation statt, der sich unserer Kontrolle entzieht und der im Grunde das widerspiegelt, was auch beim Prozess des „Machens" vor sich geht.

Geht es – wenn jemand Schmuck trägt – um Grundprinzipien, Statements, Konzepte oder wissenschaftlich hergeleitete Äußerungen? Möchte deshalb jemand ein Schmuckstück tragen? Oder geht es darum, dass jemand es trägt, weil sie oder er berührt ist? Entsteht diese Berührung durch die Intensität des Machens? Oder die Schlüssigkeit des Konzepts? Oder die Vermittlung von Status? Oder die Schönheit der Form? In dem Moment, in dem jemand Schmuck anlegt, wird das Stück zu ihrem oder seinem Stück. Worum es der Trägerin oder dem Träger geht, entzieht sich dem Einfluss aller anderen.

Auszug aus der Einführungsrede zur Ausstellung nsaio[5] in der Landesvertretung Rheinland-Pfalz, Berlin, am 12. Juni 2014

take another look at what has happened. To rethink what I have heard or seen. An attempt to clarify, to find the essence, or perhaps to simply empty one's head in order to be able to think about things again with detachment. A time that may be needed for recognising what things are disturbing or unimportant.

On adornment
Our students have chosen to make jewellery because they find in it a medium which enables them 'to speak' with it. And I am very enthusiastic about the fact that there is often an 'understanding' when someone looks at pieces of jewellery or buys them. But the moment someone wants to know more, wants to return to the usual plane of language, when an explanation is demanded for what that is now, when an explanation is demanded for what idea underpins it, when an explanation is demanded for why that is now touching, part of a question always remains unanswered. After all, speaking is often reduced to affirming a formal choice. It cannot convey everything that feeling has chosen. Ultimately a residual communication takes place that eludes our control and basically reflects what also goes on in the process of 'making'.

Are fundamental principles, statements, concepts or utterances grounded in science – when someone is wearing jewellery – at stake? Are those the reasons why someone would like to wear a piece of jewellery? Or is it about someone wearing it because s/he is moved by it? Is this being moved caused by the intensity of making? Or the consistency of the concept? Or the status it confers? Or the beauty of its form? The moment someone puts on jewellery, that piece becomes his or her piece. What the man or woman wearing it is concerned with in so doing evades the influence of all others.

Excerpt from the introductory talk opening the nsaio[5] exhibition at the Rhineland-Palatinate State Representative Building, Berlin, on 12 June 2014

Edelsteine im Schmuck: zwischen Bling-Bling und Kunst[1]

Wilhelm Lindemann

Vom magischen Objekt zum glitzernden Beiwerk

Die frühesten Zeugnisse menschlicher Bearbeitung von Edelsteinen reichen bis ins 7. Jahrtausend v. Chr. zurück. Die Kulturgeschichte des Edelsteins als Schmuckstein im heutigen Sinne beginnt im Okzident hingegen erst in der frühen Neuzeit. Bis dahin hatte er vor allem magisch-rituelle oder religiös-kultische Funktionen, wurde als Siegel verwendet oder in der Medizin eingesetzt. Plinius der Ältere (ca. 23–79 n. Chr.) verurteilt in seiner *Naturkunde* nachdrücklich den profanen Gebrauch von Edelsteinen als Luxus, der die Strafe der Götter herausfordere.[2] Der oströmische Kaiser Konstantin der Große (270/288–337 n. Chr.) bedroht das Tragen „magischer Gemmen" sogar mit dem Tod durch Enthaupten.[3] Sein Nachfolger Leo I. (reg. 457–474) erlässt im *Codex Justinianus* kaiserliche Reservatsrechte für das Tragen von Edelsteinen.[4] Damit beginnt die Geschichte des Edelsteins als Symbol gottgegebener staatlicher Herrschaft. Im Mittelalter kehrt der Edelstein als Symbol der Göttlichkeit in den religiösen Ritus zurück und erfährt in Kelchen, Monstranzen und Reliquiaren selbst eine Heiligung. Persönliche Eitelkeit und Luxus gelten in der römisch-christlichen Tradition als Sünde.

Erst mit der Renaissance beginnt die Geschichte des Edelsteins im profanen Schmuck: Plinius stellte als abschreckendes Beispiel für die verhängnisvollen Folgen von Luxus eine Version des Prometheus-Mythos vor, der Prometheus als den „Erfinder des Rings" einführt: Das Kettenglied, mit dem Prometheus an den Kaukasus gefesselt wurde, steht darin für den Fingerring und der Fels für den Edelstein.[5] Die Renaissance-Version des Mythos weist in eine neue Richtung: In der Konzeption des Vincenzo Borghini (1515–1580) für das Deckengemälde im Studiolo des Palazzo Vecchio heißt es zum Erfinder des Schmucksteins: „Dabei soll [...] die Natur gemalt werden, und als ihr Begleiter Prometheus, der, wie Plinius sagt, Erfinder der kostbaren Steine und Ringe war, und der der Sage nach, als er am Kaukasus angekettet war, trotz seiner Leiden, mit unendlichem Fleiß sich bemüht hat, Diamanten und andere Edelsteine zu bearbeiten."[6]

---

1 Vgl. hierzu auch Wilhelm Lindemann (Hg.), *Edelstein | Kunst. Renaissance bis heute*, Stuttgart 2016.
2 C. Plinius Secundus d.Ä., *Naturkunde – Naturalis historia*, Bd. XXVII, hg. und übersetzt von Roderich König in Zusammenarbeit mit Joachim Hopp, München 1994, S. 16–27.
3 Simone Michel, *Die magischen Gemmen. Zu Bildern und Zauberformeln auf geschnittenen Steinen der Antike und Neuzeit*, Berlin 2004, S. 232.
4 Siehe Gerda Friess, *Edelsteine im Mittelalter. Wandel und Kontinuität in ihrer Bedeutung durch zwölf Jahrhunderte*, Hildesheim 1980, S. 59f.
5 C. Plinius Secundus d.Ä., a.a.O., S. 16f.

Gemstones in Jewellery: between Bling and Art[1]

Wilhelm Lindemann

From magical object to glittering accessory

The earliest evidence of humans working with gemstones goes back to the seventh century BCE. The history of gemstones being used as jewellery in the West, however, doesn't begin until the early modern era. Up until then, the function of gemstones fell mainly under the magical/ritualistic or religious/cult categories; they were engraved for use as seals or employed in medicine. In his *Natural History*, Pliny the Elder (c. 23–79 CE) expressly judged the secular use of gemstones as a luxury that begged for divine retribution.[2] Constantine the Great (270/288–337 CE), ruler of the Byzantine Empire, threatened to behead anyone wearing 'magical gems'.[3] His successor, Leo I (reign: 457–474), ensured in the *Codex Justinianus* that only emperors had the right to wear gemstones.[4] Thus began the history of the gemstone as a symbol of the divine right of kings. In the Middle Ages gemstones returned to religious rituals as a symbol of divinity, becoming sacred through their use in chalices, monstrances and reliquaries. Personal vanity and luxury were considered sins in the Roman Catholic tradition.

It was not until the Renaissance that the history of the gemstone in secular jewellery began: Pliny introduced a warning about the calamitous consequences of luxury in a version of the Prometheus myth that proposed Prometheus as the 'inventor of the ring'. The chain link that fastened Prometheus to the Caucasus represented the type of ring worn on a finger, and the rock stood for the gemstone.[5] The Renaissance version of this myth pointed in a new direction: in his concept for the mural on the ceiling of the Studiolo in the Palazzo Vecchio, Vincenzo Borghini (1515–1580) said of the inventor of the jewel, 'Here […] nature should be painted, and its companion should be Prometheus, who, as Pliny says, invented decorative stones and rings, and, according to the legend, when he was chained to the Caucasus, he worked assiduously on diamonds and other gemstones, despite his suffering.'[6]

---

1 For more on this, see also Wilhelm Lindemann (ed.), *Gemstone | Art. Renaissance to the Present Day*, Stuttgart 2016.
2 C. Plinius Secundus, *Naturkunde. Naturalis historia*, vol. XXVII, ed. and trans. Roderich König in collaboration with Joachim Hopp, Munich 1994, pp. 16–27.
3 Simone Michel, *Die magischen Gemmen. Zu Bildern und Zauberformeln auf geschnittenen Steinen der Antike und Neuzeit*, Berlin 2004, p. 232.
4 See Gerda Friess, *Edelsteine im Mittelalter. Wandel und Kontinuität in ihrer Bedeutung durch zwölf Jahrhunderte*, Hildesheim 1980, pp. 59–60.
5 C. Plinius Secundus 1994 (see note 2), pp. 16–17.

Mit der Renaissance beginnt sich ein neues Schmuckverständnis durchzusetzen, in dem der Schmuck, entkleidet von seinen magisch-religiösen Verweisen, zum Werkzeug im profanen Kult an der Schönheit wird. Leon Battista Alberti weist ihm dabei eine rein ornamentale Funktion zur Verzierung seiner Trägerin oder seines Trägers zu. Mit Bezug auf die Jünglinge von Athen bei Cicero schreibt er: „Bei ihnen wäre [...] die Anwendung von Schmuck sehr vorteilhaft gewesen; durch Färben und Verdecken aller etwaigen Unförmigkeiten, durch Kämmen und Glätten wären sie schöner geworden, so dass das Unerwünschte weniger abgestoßen und das Anmutige mehr ergötzt hätte. Sind wir davon überzeugt, so wird der Schmuck gleichsam ein die Schönheit unterstützender Schimmer und etwa deren Ergänzung sein. Daraus erhellt [...], dass die Schönheit gleichsam dem schönen Körper eingeboren ist und ihn ganz durchdringt, der Schmuck aber mehr die Natur erdichteten Scheines und äußerer Zutat habe als innerlicher Art sei".[7] Schmuck wird zum Zierrat, aber auch zum Repräsentationsobjekt für Reichtum und Geschmack.

Ab der Mitte des 14. Jahrhunderts beginnen die Schleifer, die zuvor lediglich als Cabochons gemugelten Edelsteine in eine facettierte Form zu bringen. Dieser frühe Tafelschliff wird bis zirka 1700 zunächst vornehmlich im burgundisch-französischen Raum zu seiner geradezu ikonischen Gestalt des runden Brillanten weiterentwickelt. Diese gilt bis heute im Juwelenschmuck als die Idealform des Edelsteins und hat das Bild des Edelsteins in einer solchen Weise geprägt, dass sie von Laien sogar vielfach als die natürliche Form des Kristalls angesehen wird. Für die Herausbildung der Form waren keineswegs optische Aspekte maßgeblich, sie resultiert eher aus der pythagoreisch-euklidischen Proportionenlehre und einer neuplatonischen Kosmologie, die den Zeitgeist und die Ästhetik der Renaissance prägten. Ernest Babelon (1854–1924) berichtet in seiner *Histoire de la gravure sur gemmes en France*, es habe Mitte des 17. Jahrhunderts in Paris keine Edelsteingraveure mehr gegeben, da die Steinschneidekunst durch die Mode des Schliffs facettierter Schmucksteine vollständig verdrängt worden sei.[8] Deshalb habe sich Ludwig XIV. gezwungen gesehen, einen Graveur zur Ausbildung im Steinschnitt nach Florenz zu schicken, um Frankreich unabhängig von den Gemmen-Importen aus dem Ausland, vornehmlich aus Norditalien, zu machen.

---

6   Marco Dezzi Bardeschi u.a., *Lo Stanzino del Principe in Palazzo Vecchio: i concetti, le immagini, il desiderio*, Firenze: Palazzo Vecchio, 1570 – Forti di Belvedere 1980, Florenz 1980, zit. nach: Gernot Böhme, Hartmut Böhme, *Feuer, Wasser, Erde, Luft. Eine Kulturgeschichte der Elemente*, München 1996, S. 15.
7   Leon Battista Alberti, *Zehn Bücher über die Baukunst*, Darmstadt 1975, S. 293f.
8   Ernest Babelon, *Histoire de la gravure sur gemmes en France: depuis les origines jusqu'à l'époque contemporaine*, Paris 1902, S. 151.

During the Renaissance a new understanding of jewellery began to assert itself, according to which jewellery, relieved of its magical, religious references, became an instrument in the secular cult of beauty. Leon Battista Alberti endowed it with a purely ornamental function, a way of decorating its wearer. Referring to the youths of Athens in Cicero, he writes, 'In this case [...] had ornament been applied by painting and masking anything ugly, or by grooming and polishing the attractive, it would have had the effect of making the displeasing less offensive and the pleasing more delightful. If this is conceded, ornament may be defined as a form of auxiliary light and complement to beauty. From this it follows [...] that beauty is some inherent property, to be found suffused all through the body of that which may be called beautiful; whereas ornament, rather than being inherent, has the character of something attached or additional.'[7] Jewellery became an embellishment as well as an object representing wealth and taste.

In the mid-fourteenth century gemstone cutters, who previously had shaped gems into simple cabochons, began faceting stones. Mainly used in the Burgundian/French lands, the early table cut had already developed into the practically iconic shape of the round brilliant around 1700. To this day the brilliant cut is considered the ideal shape for a gemstone; it has influenced the gemstone's image so much that laypeople often think that it is the natural shape of a crystal. This shape did not evolve for optical reasons; rather, it is the result of Pythagorean/Euclidean theories of proportion and a Neo-Platonic cosmology that characterised the zeitgeist and the aesthetics of the Renaissance. In his *Histoire de la gravure sur gemmes en France* Ernest Babelon (1854–1924) reports that there were no more gemstone engravers in Paris in the mid-seventeenth century, because the fashion for faceted cuts had completely erased the art of engraving them.[8] Louis XIV was thus compelled to send an engraver to Florence to be further educated in gemstone engraving so that France would no longer have to rely upon gems imported from abroad, mainly from northern Italy.

As the fashion for faceted ornamental stones radiated from the French court, a secular concept of jewellery emerged; primarily intended to serve the decorative cult of beauty surrounding the wearer, the concept has lasted to this day. At the same time the development of geometrically defined faceting

6   Marco Dezzi Bardeschi et al., *Lo Stanzino del Principe in Palazzo Vecchio, i concetti, le immagini, il desiderio, Firenze: Palazzo Vecchio 1570/Forti di Belvedere 1980*, Florence 1980, quoted in: Gernot Böhme and Hartmut Böhme, *Feuer, Wasser, Erde, Luft. Eine Kulturgeschichte der Elemente*, Munich 1996, p. 15.
7   Leon Battista Alberti, *On the Art of Building in Ten Books*, trans. Joseph Rykwert, Neil Leach and Robert Tavernor, Cambridge, MA, 1988, p. 156.
8   Ernest Babelon, *Histoire de la gravure sur gemmes en France: depuis les origines jusqu'à l'époque contemporaine*, Paris 1902, p. 151.

Die vom französischen Hof ausstrahlende Mode facettierter Schmucksteine gab der Herausbildung eines profanen Schmuckverständnisses, das vor allem dem dekorativen Kult an der Schönheit der Schmuckträgerin oder des Schmuckträgers zu dienen hatte, bis in die Gegenwart wirkende Impulse. Gleichzeitig bereitete sich mit der Entwicklung geometrisch definierter Schliffformen und den daraus resultierenden Normierungen die vorindustrielle Massenproduktion von Schmuck vor. Bereits unter Ludwig XIV. unternahm man in Frankreich erhebliche Anstrengungen zu einer Reform der bislang ständischen beruflichen Ausbildung. Sie führte im frühen 18. Jahrhundert schließlich zur Gründung von kostenlosen Zeichenschulen für die verschiedenen Graveursberufe, in denen – unter dem Aspekt der Gestaltung – vor allem eine Standardisierung der Schönheitsvorstellungen durch das Kopieren von Vorlagen erfolgte. Nach dem Vorbild der Pariser Zeichenschulen wurden in der Folge in ganz Europa Akademien gegründet, im Jahre 1772 beispielsweise die Staatliche Zeichenakademie Hanau. Von diesen Keimzellen außerbetrieblicher Goldschmiedeausbildung geht bis heute ein großer Einfluss auf den Schmuck aus.

Die im Barock beginnende weitgehende Festlegung auf einen Kanon idealer Schliffformen war Grundlage für die industrielle Massenproduktion von facettierten Schmucksteinen. Sie wurden bis in die Gegenwart – vor allem zur Optimierung der Lichtreflexion – nur noch geringfügig weiterentwickelt. Die industrielle Produktionsweise machte ab dem 19. Jahrhundert die Zertifizierung von Edelsteinen immer dringlicher, um einem drohenden Verfall der Marktpreise entgegenzuwirken. Erst infolge der Meterkonvention von 1875 wurde das metrische Karat einheitlich als Gewichtsmaß für Edelsteine festgelegt. Mit der Transformation des Proletariats in wirtschaftlich potente Konsumentinnen und Konsumenten werden Edelsteine im 20. Jahrhundert zu wohlfeilen Massenartikeln. Um auf ihre Trägerin und ihren Träger abstrahlen zu können, muss ihr exklusiver Nimbus vor allem durch Marketingstrategien gestützt werden, die auf zertifizierter Wertigkeit basieren.

Ab dem frühen 20. Jahrhundert setzt die Produktion synthetischer Edelsteine im industriellen Maßstab den Markt für natürliche Edelsteine erheblich unter Druck.[9] Um den Marktwert zu stabilisieren, werden in der Echtheitszertifizierung daher immer subtilere kristallographische Untersuchungsverfahren eingeführt. Die Zertifizierung von Edelsteinen, insbesondere von Diamanten, erfolgt heute nach den Kriterien der „4 Cs" (Carat, Colour, Clarity und Cut) und erweckt den Anschein größtmöglicher Objektivität auf naturwissenschaftlicher Basis. Da im Vordergrund der Wertbemessung quantifizierende physi-

---

9 Vgl. hierzu Elisabeth Vaupel, „Edelsteine aus der Fabrik", in: *Technikgeschichte*, Jahrgang 82 (2015), Heft 4, S. 273–302.

and the resulting standardisation prepared the way for the pre-industrial mass production of jewellery. Even under Louis XIV considerable effort was made in France to reform the existing system of education in trades. In the early eighteenth century this ultimately led to the founding of free schools of drawing for the various types of engravers. There, under the aspect of design, copying source materials contributed to the standardisation of certain ideas of beauty. Consequently, academies based on the Parisian model of drawing schools were founded throughout Europe. One of these was the State Drawing Academy in Hanau in 1772. Out of these nucleuses arose training for goldsmiths outside of the trade, and this training continues to exercise a great deal of influence on ornamental jewellery today.

A canon of ideal gemstone shapes widely established in the Baroque era became the foundation for industrial mass production of faceted gemstones. These basic forms were only marginally altered, primarily to optimise the reflection of light. From the nineteenth century onwards industrial production methods made it even more important to certify gemstones in order to counteract a dangerous decline in market prices. It was not until after the metric convention of 1875 that the metric carat was established as the common weight for gemstones. As the proletariat transformed into economically potent consumers, gemstones became in the twentieth century inexpensive, mass-produced items. In order to increase their power to enhance the wearer, their halo of exclusivity had to be bolstered, primarily by marketing strategies based on certified value.

From the early twentieth century onwards synthetic gemstones produced according to industry standards added considerable pressure to the market for natural gemstones.[9] To stabilise their market value, certificates of authenticity began to encompass ever more subtle processes for scrutinising crystals. Today gemstones (especially diamonds) are evaluated according to the 'four Cs': carat, colour, clarity and cut, kindling the appearance of the greatest possible science-based objectivity. Because quantifying criteria, such as weight, purity and overall reflection of light (cut), are important to assessing value, the aesthetic qualities of the material, such as inclusions, fractures and so forth, vanish from sight. The ephemeral reflection of light that can be seen by the naked eye requires a certificate of authenticity in order to guarantee the stability of the gem's material value. It secures the owner's luxurious sense of pleasure in the object's value. Sparkling gemstones are conquering modern jewellery, regardless of whether they were unaffordable multi-carat diamonds

---

9   For more on this, see Elisabeth Vaupel, 'Edelsteine aus der Fabrik', *Technikgeschichte*, vol. 82 (2015), issue 4, pp. 273–302.

kalische Kriterien wie Gewicht, Reinheit und Totalreflexion des Lichts (Schliff) stehen, geraten ästhetische Qualitäten des Materials, wie sie beispielsweise bei Einschlüssen, Brüchen usw. sichtbar werden, aus dem Blick. Der mit bloßem Auge erkennbare ephemere Lichtreflex erfordert das Echtheitszertifikat, um die materielle Wertbeständigkeit zu garantieren. Es sichert den luxuriösen Genusswert für den Eigentümer. Funkelnde Edelsteine erobern den Schmuck der Neuzeit: ob als unerschwinglicher mehrkarätiger Diamant, als mit bloßem Auge kaum noch erkennbarer, industriell gefertigter Winzling – oder als Imitat aus gefärbtem Glas.

Die ungeliebte Ikone

In der zeitgenössischen Schmuckkunst, soweit sie sich selbst als „Autorenschmuck" apostrophiert, spielt der Edelstein bislang eine eher marginale Rolle. Die Schmuckszene hat ihn bis in die jüngste Gegenwart weitgehend ignoriert. Nicht einmal die Tatsache, dass der brillant geschliffene Kristall seit dem Barock eine zunehmende stilprägende Funktion im „Juwelenschmuck" einnahm – und als Imitat auch den Modeschmuck prägt –, ist den meisten Protagonistinnen und Protagonisten eine Auseinandersetzung wert. Nur wenige herausragende Schmuckkünstlerinnen und -künstler wie Friedrich Becker haben den Edelstein als Werkstoff interpretiert, an dem sich der eigene Wille zur Gestaltung entzündet. Erst seit den frühen 1970er-Jahren setzt, beginnend mit Bernd Munsteiner, eine Renaissance im Verständnis des Edelsteins als Material der Kunst ein, die sich in wachsendem Maße auch im Schmuck niederschlägt. Sie entfaltet heute, vor allem inspiriert und vorangetrieben durch die Arbeit der Hochschule Trier, Fachrichtung Edelstein und Schmuck in Idar-Oberstein, auch eine zunehmend internationale Ausstrahlung, die über das Werk einzelner Edelsteinkünstlerinnen und -künstler hinausgeht.

Ausschlaggebend für die negative Einstellung gegenüber dem Edelstein im Autorenschmuck dürften mehrere Gründe gewesen sein:

- Fast alle Künstlerinnen und Künstler des „Autorenschmucks" stehen in einer goldschmiedischen Tradition und verfügen über keine eigene handwerkliche Kompetenz in der Edelsteinbearbeitung. Sie sind Abnehmerinnen und Abnehmer industriell oder handwerklich gefertigter Steine, die, zu kanonisierten Schliffen normiert, das ikonische Bild des funkelnden Edelsteines realisieren. Der vorproduzierte Schmuckstein erscheint in seiner Perfektion ebenso unnahbar wie unangreifbar. Wegen seines starken optischen Auftritts, der das Werk der Goldschmiedin oder des Goldschmieds oftmals überstrahlt, droht er dieses latent auf die Funktion einer Edelsteinfassung zu reduzieren.

or tiny, industrially faceted stones that can barely be seen by the naked eye – or imitations made of coloured glass.

The unloved icon

To the extent that it's apostrophised as 'auteur' or 'designer' jewellery, in contemporary jewellery the gemstone has played a rather marginal role. Jewellery designers have widely ignored it until very recently. Not even the fact that the faceted crystal has exercised increasing influence upon 'ornamental jewellery' ever since the Baroque era – while its imitation has also influenced costume jewellery – has made it worth exploring for most of the major figures on the scene. Only a few outstanding artisanal jewellers, such as Friedrich Becker, have regarded the gemstone as a material that inspires creativity. It was not until the early 1970s that artists, starting with Bernd Munsteiner, began a renaissance based on a concept of the gemstone as a material for art, which has gradually come to have more influence over jewellery. It continues to unfold today – mainly inspired and fuelled by the work being done at the Department of Gemstones and Jewellery at the Trier University of Applied Sciences in Idar-Oberstein – and is beginning to radiate outwards on an increasingly international scale, going beyond the work of individual jewellers.

There are probably more reasons for the negative attitude towards the gemstone among artisanal jewellers:

- Nearly all artisanal jewellers are trained in traditional goldsmithing and have no training in cutting gemstones. They acquire industrially produced or hand-cut stones whose cuts conform to canonised shapes so that they embody the iconic image of the sparkling gemstone. In their perfection, pre-fabricated ornamental stones seem as unapproachable as they are untouchable. Due to the gemstone's strong appearance, which often outshines the work of the goldsmith, it threatens to subtly reduce the piece to the function of a gemstone setting.
- Industrially produced stones are made in accordance with a concept of ornamental jewellery that fundamentally contradicts the artistic ambitions and statements of artisanal jewellers. The majority of them are rooted in the critical traditions of twentieth-century art and therefore distance themselves from ornamentation; the ornament is merely used as a citation, or with deconstructivist, critical intentions.
- In addition, the sparkling stone resists further creative development, and not simply because of its conceptual and technical perfection, which has evolved over the centuries. Each change made by the artist robs the stone of its effect and, hence, of its 'inherent sense'.

- Die industriell gefertigten Steine verfolgen ein ornamentales Schmuckkonzept, das in einem grundsätzlichen Widerspruch zu den künstlerischen Ambitionen und Aussagen der Produzentinnen und Produzenten des Autorenschmucks steht. Sie sind mehrheitlich in den kritischen Traditionen der Kunst des 20. Jahrhunderts verwurzelt und distanzieren sich vom Ornament; es findet lediglich als Zitat oder in dekonstruktivistisch-kritischer Absicht Verwendung.
- Zudem widersetzt sich der funkelnde Stein nicht nur wegen der über Jahrhunderte hinweg gewachsenen konzeptionellen und technischen Perfektion einer weiteren gestalterischen Bearbeitung. Jede künstlerische Veränderung beraubt ihn seines Effekts und damit zugleich seines „inneren Sinns".
- Der Edelstein ist in seiner ästhetischen Wirkung als funkelnder Lichtreflex zum Trompe-l'œil, zu einem entmaterialisierten Trugbild mutiert, das durch die Bewegung der Trägerinnen oder Träger und der Betrachterinnen oder Betrachter zu einem vermeintlichen Leben erweckt wird. Nur in dieser besonderen Form, als gleichsam immaterieller Lichtreflex, ist er sich selbst treu. Indem der Stein als Material gleichsam hinter seinem funkelnden Schein verschwindet, wird er als gestaltbares Material obsolet. Der funkelnde Glanz wird zum irrlichtigen Trugbild einer auf den oberflächlichen Effekt und nicht auf eine innere Werteordnung orientierten Weltsicht.
- Edelsteine werden nicht zuletzt aufgrund der Vermarktungsstrategien der Industrie heute hauptsächlich als Luxusgüter interpretiert – auch wenn ein Großteil eher in einem niedrigpreisigen Marktsegment gehandelt wird und insofern nur einen schwachen Abglanz der Aura des Luxus repräsentiert. Die Autorinnen und Autoren wie auch die Käuferinnen und Käufer des zeitgenössischen Künstlerschmucks stehen in der Mehrheit allen Formen des ostentativen Konsums und des Luxus kritisch bis ablehnend gegenüber. Kritisiert wird nicht allein, dass dieses Konzept weder dem symbolischen Wert von Schmuck (als einer anthropologischen Konstante) noch der überragenden kulturhistorischen Bedeutung von Edelsteinen gerecht wird. Inakzeptabel erscheint auch die auf Naturausbeutung und Verschwendung von Ressourcen basierende Gestik: Die auf Ewigkeit und Wertigkeit verweisende Symbolik des Edelsteins wird durch sie konterkariert, ja geradezu ins Lächerliche gezogen. Ganz im Sinne der europäischen Tradition, die die Luxuria als eine der sieben Todsünden verurteilt und sie in der Gesellschaft der Vanitas sieht, muss insbesondere angesichts der drohenden ökologischen Katastrophe der ausbeuterische Umgang mit Naturstoffen besonders kritisch betrachtet werden.

- Due to its aesthetic effect as a glittering reflection of light, the gemstone has become a *trompe-l'oeil*, mutating into a dematerialised illusion supposedly brought to life as the wearer and observer moves about. It is only in this special form – a practically intangible reflection of light – that it is true to itself. To the extent that the stone itself seems to disappear behind its sparkling surface, it becomes obsolete as a material for creativity. Its glittering sparkle becomes a will-o'-the-wisp illusion of a superficial effect, not of a world view based on an order of inherent values.
- Today gemstones are mainly thought of as luxury goods, not least because of the industry's marketing strategies, even though a large number of stones tend to be traded in the low-priced market segment, and in this respect they merely represent a distant echo of a luxurious aura. In the main, both makers and sellers of contemporary artisanal jewellery are either critical of, or reject, all forms of ostentatious consumption and luxury. And the critique doesn't simply focus on the fact that this concept doesn't do justice to the symbolic value of jewellery (as an anthropological constant) or to the outstanding cultural, historical significance of gemstones. Gestures based on the exploitation of nature and the squandering of resources also seem unacceptable. It counteracts – even ridicules – the symbolism of the gemstone, which represents eternity and value. Entirely in keeping with European tradition, which judges Luxuria as one of the seven deadly sins and regards it as part of a vain society, exploitive treatment of natural resources has to be considered from a particularly critical point of view, especially considering the looming threat of ecological catastrophe.
- Uncalibrated, industrially manufactured stones, on the other hand, are burdened by the gemstone cutter's imprint to such a degree that it is difficult to do the work on them that is required to turn them into an autonomous work of art. Their own aesthetic messages provide a strong precept that stands in the way of the jeweller's ability to express his or her own position.

The renaissance of the gemstone in auteur jewellery

The gemstone's renaissance in contemporary jewellery began, also from a global point of view, in Europe's gemstone centre, Idar-Oberstein. Impulses for this arose in the early 1970s, primarily from Bernd Munsteiner. At the heart of the gemstone's rebirth is its rediscovery as a material that can be creatively shaped by artists. Munsteiner broke with the kind of traditional polishing and cutting associated with faceting to develop an abstract formal vocabulary orientat-

- Nichtkalibrierte Steine aus industrieller Herstellung tragen hingegen die Handschrift der Schleiferin oder des Schleifers in einem so hohen Maße, dass sie als autonomes Kunstwerk eine Weiterverarbeitung erschweren. Ihre eigene ästhetische Botschaft gibt der Schmuckkünstlerin oder dem Schmuckkünstler eine starke Vorgabe, die der Formulierung eigener Positionen im Wege steht.

Die Renaissance des Edelsteins im Autorenschmuck

Die Renaissance des Edelsteins in der Schmuckkunst der Gegenwart hat, auch im globalen Maßstab betrachtet, vom europäischen Edelsteinzentrum Idar-Oberstein ihren Ausgang genommen. Erste Impulse hat bereits seit den frühen 1970er-Jahren vor allem Bernd Munsteiner gegeben. Im Mittelpunkt der Renaissance des Edelsteins steht die Wiederentdeckung als künstlerisch frei gestaltbares Material. Munsteiner bricht rigoros mit den Schleiftraditionen des Facettenschliffs und entwickelt eine abstrakte Formensprache, die sich an der Kunst der Moderne orientiert. Er grenzt sich damit auch klar gegen die bis in die Gegenwart vorherrschende neoklassizistisch-naturalistische Gestaltungspraxis in der Edelsteingravur ab. Vor allem aber setzt Munsteiner in seiner Arbeit die üblichen Bewertungsmaßstäbe für Edelsteine außer Kraft. Im Mittelpunkt des Werks steht das natürliche Material selbst, seine Farben, die strukturellen Merkmale seines Wuchses, seine optischen Phänomene.

Im letzten Jahrzehnt hat sich der Idar-Obersteiner Ausbildungsgang Edelstein und Schmuck unter der Ägide von Theo Smeets und Ute Eitzenhöfer als kreatives Zentrum dieser Renaissance des Edelsteins auch international etabliert. Im Mittelpunkt des Studiums steht dabei nicht die handwerkliche Ausbildung in der Bearbeitung des Materials – was keineswegs heißt, dass der praktische Umgang mit dem Stein im Schleifatelier vernachlässigt wird. Doch geht es vor allem um die ästhetischen Qualitäten des Materials, die experimentelle Auslotung seiner physikalischen Eigenschaften, seiner Gestaltungspotenziale sowie seiner Wirkung in Relation zu anderen Werkstoffen und insbesondere zum menschlichen Körper. Ein inhaltlicher Schwerpunkt des Studiums liegt auch im Bereich der Reflexion des gesellschaftlichen Kontextes rund um den Edelstein. In den Diskurs einbezogen sind dabei nicht nur die sozialen und ökonomischen Rahmenbedingungen des Schmuckmarktes, sondern auch grundsätzliche ethische Fragen, insbesondere zur moralischen Verantwortung des Künstlers in der Gesellschaft.

Dieser Diskurs führt zu einem völlig neuen Blick auf den Edelstein: er wird als Naturgegenstand wiederentdeckt und vor dem Hintergrund der ökologischen Krise im Sinne eines von Verantwortung geprägten Naturbewusstseins

ed towards modern art. In this way, he also clearly distances himself from the neo-classicist, naturalist practice of design common to gemstone engraving, which remains predominant to this day. Above all, though, Munsteiner dismisses the usual standards for assessing gemstones. At the heart of his work is the natural material itself – its colours, the structural characteristics of its growth, its optical phenomena.

Over the last decade the Department of Gemstones and Jewellery in Idar-Oberstein, under the auspices of Theo Smeets and Ute Eitzenhöfer, has also established itself internationally as a creative centre for the gemstone renaissance. Training in the craft of working with the material is not at the heart of the programme – which in no way means that the practical craft of working with gemstones in the studio is neglected. Yet, it is mainly about the aesthetic qualities of the material, the experimental exploration of its physical characteristics, its potential for shaping and its effect on other materials, especially the human body. Another focus of the programme lies in reflecting upon the social context surrounding the gemstone. Included in the discourse are both the social and economic frameworks of the jewellery market, as well as fundamental ethical questions, especially those pertaining to the artist's moral responsibility to society.

This discourse leads to a completely new view of the gemstone. It's been rediscovered as a natural object and interpreted in front of the backdrop of the ecological crisis, in the sense that an awareness of nature should be characterised by fostering responsibility towards it. Therefore, gemstones as natural objects are frequently only processed a little bit and presented as precious *objets trouvés*. It's about a new treatment of the gemstone as a material for jewellery, on two counts. First, artistic concepts are discussed and realised as ornamentation. These concepts reflect upon the world of glamorous jewellery in a critical way and, going beyond jewellery, explore the ways that nature is exploited to create luxury goods. They are also considered artistic, political statements. Gemstones are a natural symbol for the world of consumerism and waste, and they are put into positions in relation to the world that are polemic, citational, ironic or revealing. In this context a deconstructivist approach is taken, especially to the process of faceting, which functions as a citation or reference to the practice of ornamentation.

The second and more fundamental consequence derived from this mainly critical reflection is a complete re-evaluation of the gemstone as a material. As a natural object, it symbolises the sublimity of nature, which transcends the temporality of human existence and thus simultaneously refers to its foundations and limitations. In this updating of the memento mori, the gemstone

interpretiert. Nicht selten werden Edelsteine als Naturgegenstände daher nur in geringem Maße bearbeitet und wie ein kostbares *objet trouvé* inszeniert. Es geht um einen in doppelter Hinsicht neuen Umgang mit dem Edelstein als Material im Schmuck: Zum einen werden durchaus als Schmuck tragbare künstlerische Konzepte diskutiert und umgesetzt. Diese reflektieren die Welt des glamourösen Schmucks kritisch und setzen sich – über den Schmuck hinaus – mit dem luxuriösen Gebrauch und der Vernutzung von Natur auseinander. Sie verstehen sich auch als künstlerisch-politisches Statement. Edelsteine stehen dabei als Natursymbol einer Welt des Konsumismus und der Verschwendung gegenüber, zu der sie sich mal polemisch, mal zitierend, ironisierend oder entlarvend in Position bringen. Verbreitet ist in diesem Kontext ein dekonstruktivistischer Umgang vor allem mit dem Facettenschliff, der als Zitat oder Verweis auf die ornamentale Praxis fungiert.

Als zweite und grundsätzlichere Konsequenz aus dieser vor allem kritischen Reflexion resultiert eine völlige Neubewertung des Edelsteins als Material: Als Naturgegenstand steht er symbolisch für die Erhabenheit der Natur schlechthin, die die Zeitlichkeit der menschlichen Existenz transzendiert und damit gleichzeitig auf deren Grundlagen und Begrenztheit verweist. Mit dieser Aktualisierung des menschlichen Memento mori spricht der Edelstein die Verantwortung des Menschen für eine ihm gegebene Natur an. Edelsteine erscheinen hier also nicht mehr als rationalistisches Symbol der beherrschten Natur wie beim Brillantschliff, sondern als kostbares Geschenk der Natur. Dabei wird in vielfältiger Weise das natürliche Erscheinungsbild des Materials inszeniert, wobei auch der formen- und strukturreiche Auftritt opaker Farbsteine wie zum Beispiel des Achats oder des Jaspis zu neuer Wertschätzung gelangt.

Im Ergebnis zeigt sich eine völlig gewandelte Funktion des Edelsteins im Schmuck: Sie reicht vom frühen magisch-rituellen oder religiös-kultischen Fetisch über das neuzeitliche, auf eine dekorative Funktion reduzierte Ornament bis hin zum kommunikativen Element im Schmuck: Es ist eine Botschaft, die an die Betrachterin und den Betrachter des Edelsteinschmucks adressiert wird und die zum Gespräch herausfordert. Es ist aber auch ein Bekenntnis der Schmuckträgerin oder des Schmuckträgers zu einer inhaltlichen Position, das nicht nur einen Standpunkt kommuniziert, sondern zugleich auch eigene Identität stiftet.

addresses humankind's responsibility towards nature, which is taken for granted. Here, gemstones no longer appear to be rationalist symbols of a restrained nature, as the brilliant cut is; rather, they are a precious gift of nature. Here, the natural appearance of the material is presented in various ways, through which the appearance of opaque, coloured stones that are full of different shapes and textures (such as agate or jasper) takes on new value.

Ultimately, one can perceive that gemstones now have a fully altered function in ornamentation. This function covers ground, from the early, magical/ritualistic or religious/cult fetish to the modern ornament reduced to a decorative function, all the way to the communicative element of jewellery. It is a message addressed to those who look at gemstone jewellery, and it challenges them to engage in a conversation. Yet, it is also the wearer's confession of a contextual position that not only communicates a point of view but also lends the wearer identity at the same time.

Schmuck im Kontext

Marjan Unger

Schmuck ist ein Ausdruck der elementaren menschlichen Neigung zur Dekoration und Verzierung. Schmuckstücke symbolisieren die Freude am Leben und entsprechen dem Bedürfnis nach Zeichen, mit denen wir uns anderen Menschen zeigen und der Welt entgegentreten können. Schon zu Urzeiten ließ sich dieser innere Drang durch schöne Muscheln, einen besonderen Stein, ein paar Blüten oder die Zähne eines wilden Tieres befriedigen. Schmuck gehört zum Menschen und existiert vermutlich solange wie die Menscheit.

Die Proportionen des menschlichen Körpers bestimmen die Größe des Schmucks. In den meisten Fällen sind Schmuckstücke kleinformatige Objekte mit unzähligen Bedeutungen. Über die Jahrhunderte wurden sämtliche Begierden, Bürden und Ängste des Menschen darin verkörpert: Schmuck ist erotisch, pragmatisch, strahlt Macht aus, besänftigt übersinnliche Kräfte, spiegelt die Liebe zum Natürlichen, zu einer bestimmten Person, steht für Trauer und das Streben nach Schönheit. Jede Epoche erzeugt ihre eigenen Botschaften, bei denen es sich zumeist um Variationen dieser universellen Bedeutungen handelt.

Nicht immer fallen Schmuckstücke sofort ins Auge. Weil sie der Haut nah und im Allgemeinen nur aus kurzer Distanz zu würdigen sind, besitzen sie eine gewisse Intimität. Es widerspricht den Konventionen unserer Kultur, diese Intimität allzu sehr zu verletzen.

Das Spannende an Schmuckstücken ist die Dialektik zwischen ihrer Intimität und dem Ausmaß ihrer Botschaften.[1] Die Bündelung von Bedeutungen in winzigen Artefakten wie Ringen, Halsketten, Armbändern, Gürteln und Kopfverzierungen kann schwindelerregend sein. Das begrenzte Format nötigt den Künstlern nicht nur Präzision, Exzellenz und höchste Handwerkskunst ab, sondern reizt auch zur Impulsivität und bringt so Ornamente hervor, die oft nur wenige Stunden getragen werden.

In Schmuckpublikationen wird man selten eine Definition von Schmuck finden. Angesichts seiner universellen Natur mag es auch überflüssig erscheinen, weiter darüber nachzudenken. Die Art und Weise jedoch, wie Menschen Schmuck betrachten, ist einem ständigen Wandel unterworfen. Im Verlauf des 20. Jahrhunderts etwa sorgten weitreichende soziale und wirtschaftliche Entwicklungen dafür, dass die Funktion von Schmuck neu definiert wurde. In der westlichen Welt erhielten mehr Menschen als jemals zuvor Zugang zu Luxusgütern. Gleichzeitig wurde Schmuck zunehmend zur ausschließlich weiblichen

---

1 Graham Hughes, *Jewelry*, London 1966, S. 7: „Ihre Anziehungskraft ist universell, doch ihre Wirkung ist vertraulich."

Jewellery in Context
Marjan Unger

Jewellery is an expression of the fundamental human propensity for decoration and ornament. Pieces of jewellery symbolise the pleasure of being alive and answer to people's need for signs with which to present themselves to others and to be able to face the world. This is a compulsion that could be satisfied as early as primordial times, through nice shells, a special stone, a few flowers or the teeth of a wild animal. Jewellery is related to people and has probably been around as long as humanity.

The proportions of the human body determine the size of jewellery. More often than not, pieces of jewellery are small-sized objects that come with countless meanings. Over the centuries, all human desires, burdens and fears have been represented in jewellery: eroticism, displays of power, pragmatism and the allaying of the supernatural as well as love for what is natural, love for a specific person, grief and the pursuit of beauty. Every era generates its own messages, mostly variations on these universal meanings.

Pieces of jewellery do not always catch the eye right away. They have a certain intimacy, for they are close to the skin and in general one will be able to appreciate them only from up close. It is unconventional in our culture to infringe too much on that intimacy.

What is enthralling is the dialectic between the intimacy of jewellery and the scope of its messages.[1] The concentration of meanings in tiny artefacts such as rings, necklaces, bracelets, belts and head adornments can be mindboggling. The limited size not only invites precision, excellence and the highest level of craftsmanship, but also provokes impulsiveness and thus yields ornaments that are worn for a few hours only.

In publications on jewellery one will rarely find a definition of jewellery. Given the universal nature of jewellery, it may seem superfluous to further reflect on it. The ways in which people look at jewellery, however, are subject to constant change. In the course of the twentieth century, for instance, far-reaching social and economic developments caused shifts in the role of jewellery. In the West more people than ever gained access to luxurious goods. At the same time, jewellery was increasingly relegated to the exclusive domain of women. Strict demarcations emerged within jewellery as a discipline: the assessment of the designs and the materials used shifted, in particular in the upper echelons of the cultural domain.

1   Graham Hughes, *Jewelry*, London 1966, p. 7: 'Their appeal is universal but their impact is confidential.'

Domäne degradiert. Im Fachgebiet Schmuck entwickelten sich strenge Abgrenzungen: Die Bewertung der verwendeten Designs und Materialien veränderte sich, insbesondere in den gehobenen Sphären des Kulturbereichs.

Etymologisch ist das Wort „Juwelen", für das das Deutsche auch den allgemeineren Begriff „Schmuck" verwendet, mit dem lateinischen *iocus* verwandt, das für „Skizze", „Spiel" oder „kleine Ablenkung" steht.[2] Dieser Ursprung lässt sich in mehreren Sprachen nachweisen. Das englische *jewellery* (Schmuck) ist weiter gefasst als das einfache *jewel* (Juwel oder Edelstein), im Französischen werden *joaillerie* und *bijoux* synonym verwendet, und im Italienischen ist *gioiello* der gebräuchlichste Begriff für Schmuck. Für Viele ist ein Schmuckstück demnach ein Objekt, das Freude bereitet, was zahlreiche Publizisten im Schmuckbereich zu Recht aufgreifen, um ihre Begeisterung zu erklären. Diese wohlwollende, aber einseitige Erklärung sollte uns jedoch nicht dazu verleiten, über die oft fragwürdigen Praktiken hinwegzusehen, die mit der Gewinnung, Bearbeitung und Vermarktung der üblicherweise für die Schmuckherstellung verwendeten Materialien – der Edelmetalle und Edelsteine – verbunden sind.

Schmuckstücke erzählen vom Selbstbild des Menschen und von seinen wechselseitigen Beziehungen. Sie sind Versatzstücke, die die Identität eines Menschen aufwerten und ihn bei anderen bekannt machen sollen. Als tragbare Objekte sind sie außerordentlich gut geeignet, um die eigene Stellung in einer Gesellschaft zum Ausdruck zu bringen. Sie können sowohl Unterschiede als auch Gemeinsamkeiten zwischen Einzelnen betonen. Als Mittel, um Ängste zu zerstreuen, zeugen sie zugleich von der menschlichen Lust am Dekorieren, und sie helfen Erinnerungen wachzuhalten.

Schönheit ist nur eines der Elemente, die in unseren Wechselbeziehungen eine Rolle spielen. Sie verweist auf das Außergewöhnliche und taugt von daher kaum als greifbare Norm, um in einer bestimmten Epoche und Kultur als Maßstab hochgehalten zu werden. Wer Schönheit zum einzigen Zweck eines Schmuckstücks erklärt, reduziert es auf ein Spielzeug für leichtlebige Typen und meint damit die Frauen – denn die Vorstellung, dass Schmuck hauptsächlich für Frauen bestimmt ist, entspringt einem in jüngerer Zeit geprägten westlichen Vorurteil. Die Geschichte dagegen lehrt uns, dass auch Männer Schmuck getragen haben, der zudem oft sehr aufwendig gestaltet war.

Für das Betrachten von Schmuck nicht minder relevante Begriffe sind Dekoration, Ornament und Verzierung. Dekoration bedeutet Ausschmückung oder Auszeichnung, und ein Schmuckstück kann ohne Frage als eine Dekora-

---

2 Jan Walgrave, Hilde De Decker, Pim Westerkamp und Dorothee Meigen, *Sieraad, Symbool, Signaal* (= The Jewel. Sign and Symbol), Antwerpen 1995, S. 18.

Etymologically, the word 'jewel' is related to the Latin *iocus*, which means 'sketch', 'game', or 'small distraction'.[2] This origin can be traced in several languages. In English 'jewellery' has a wider scope than 'jewel'. In French *joaillerie* and *bijoux* are used interchangeably, in Germany people use the word *Juwelen* and the more general *Schmuck*, and in Italian the most common term is *gioiello*. To many, then, a jewel is something that gives pleasure, an aspect that many authors on jewellery rightfully embrace to explain their fascination. But this sympathetic yet one-sided explanation should not cause one to ignore all the shady practices associated with winning, working and marketing materials commonly used for making jewellery – that is, precious metals and precious stones.

Pieces of jewellery are about people's self-image and how people relate to each other. They are pieces of jigsaw puzzles to enhance people's identity and make themselves known to others. As wearable objects, they are highly suitable as means to pronounce one's position within a society. They may stress both mutual differences and similarities among individuals. As vehicles for allaying fears they also testify to the human delight in decoration, and they help to keep memories alive. Beauty is just one of the elements that feature in our mutual interactions. Beauty refers to something exceptional; as such it is quite an intangible norm to hold up as a standard in a certain era and culture. When beauty is mentioned as the singular purpose of a piece of jewellery, it is reduced to a toy for frivolous types, and that must mean for women, because the notion that jewellery is chiefly meant for women is a recent and Western prejudice. But history tells us that men have also worn jewellery and often quite elaborately.

Other concepts relevant to the study of jewellery are decoration, ornament and adornment. Decoration means embellishment or distinction, and a piece of jewellery can obviously be described as a decoration of people's outward appearances. The concept of ornament is slightly more complex. In everyday parlance 'ornament' is used as a synonym of jewellery, embellishment or decoration, but within the history of art, ornament refers to a motif and to a decorative addition to works of fine art, architecture or utensils. Adornment, in this essay, refers to all decorative elements on or added to the body: jewellery items, but also accessories and body decorations such as tattoos and piercings. In combination with decorative elements on clothing, adornment can be quite complex; in this sense, a piece of jewellery can be part of adornment.

My proposal for a definition of jewellery is: an artefact that is worn by people, as a decorative and symbolic addition to their outward appearance.

---

2   Jan Walgrave, Hilde De Decker, Pim Westerkamp and Dorothee Meigen, *Sieraad, Symbool, Signaal* (= The Jewel. Sign and Symbol), Antwerp 1995, p. 18.

tion des menschlichen Äußeren beschrieben werden. Der Ornamentbegriff ist etwas komplizierter. Im Alltagsjargon wird die Bezeichnung Ornament als Synonym für Schmuck, Verschönerung oder Dekoration verwendet, doch in der Geschichte der Kunst verweist der Begriff auf ein Motiv und eine dekorative Ergänzung zu Werken der bildenden Kunst, der Architektur oder des täglichen Bedarfs. Verzierung schließlich bezeichnet in diesem Essay alle schmückenden Elemente am oder auf dem Körper, also Schmuckgegenstände, aber auch Accessoires und Körperschmuck wie Tätowierungen und Piercings. In Kombination mit dekorativen Bestandteilen auf der Kleidung kann Verzierung sehr komplex sein und kann Schmuck, in diesem Sinne, zum Teil der Verzierung werden.

Mein Vorschlag für eine Schmuckdefinition lautet: Schmuck ist ein Artefakt, das Menschen als dekorative oder symbolische Ergänzung zu ihrer äußeren Erscheinung tragen.

Der menschliche Maßstab

Sehr wenige Menschen sind mit ihrem angeborenen Äußeren vollauf zufrieden. Nur selten werden sie voll und ganz den Normen und Gepflogenheiten entsprechen, die man ihnen beibringt, wenn sie älter werden und zur Schule gehen. Obendrein sind die Chancen gering, dass die Ideale, die sie in einem bestimmten Stadium ihres Lebens pflegen, mit der selbst geformten Wirklichkeit ihres Körpers und ihrer Persönlichkeit übereinstimmen. Dieser Umstand ist heute in vielen Bereichen zum Bestandteil heftig geführter Debatten geworden.

Die Form des menschlichen Körpers ist so komplex, dass sie sich für gewichtige Manipulationen anbietet. Der britische Modeexperte und studierte Anthropologe Ted Polhemus beschreibt diesen Prozess in einem 2007 erschienenen Ausstellungskatalog über den Schmuck von Florian Ladstaetter auf prägnante und eloquente Weise: „Wie jeder andere Naturgegenstand – nur noch mehr – hörte der menschliche Körper auf, ein Ding an sich zu sein, und wurde zum Symbol für alles, was jenseits seiner selbst existiert. Weil es unseren Vorfahren nicht ausreichte, nur zu verändern, wie wir über unseren Körper denken, ihn verstehen, erleben und sogar fühlen, machten sie sich unverzüglich daran, auch das Aussehen des menschlichen Körpers mit Farbe, Narben, Tätowierungen, Piercings, Kleidung und Ornamenten zu verwandeln. Und das seit dem Anbeginn der menschlichen Evolution. [...] Als Sinnbild, als geschmücktes Objekt wurde der Körper des Menschen so für immer seinem ‚natürlichen' Zustand entrissen."[3]

---

3 Ted Polhemus, „Text 1", in: *Les Fleurs du Mal*, Ausst.-Kat. MAK Österreichisches Museum für Angewandte Kunst, Wien 2007, o. S.

The human standard

Very few people will be fully satisfied with the outer features given to them at birth. Only seldomly will they fully correspond to the norms and customs taught to them when they grow up and go to school. Moreover, chances are slim that the ideals they cherish at a certain stage of their life will coincide with the reality of their own body and personality as fashioned by them. This concern is in fact part of fierce debates within many domains today.

The human body has a complex shape that lends itself to substantial tinkering. The British fashion expert Ted Polhemus (trained as an anthropologist) concisely and eloquently describes this process in a 2007 exhibition catalogue about the jewellery of Florian Ladstaetter: 'Like every other natural object – only more so – the human body ceased to be a thing in itself and became a symbol of everything beyond itself. Not content with transforming how we think about, understand, experience and even feel our bodies, our ancestors immediately also set about transforming the appearance of the human body with paint, scars, tattoos, piercings, clothing and ornament. And this from the very beginning of human development. [...] Symbolic, decorated, the human body was thus forever torn from its "natural" state.'[3]

How people deal with their body and judge the body of others varies over time and from one culture to the next. Notions about the nude body are often determined by ideals regarding outer beauty prevalent in some period rather than by an anatomically correct representation of or a medically responsible approach to the body. This is shown, for instance, from the representation of nudes in the history of the fine arts. At times when fashion prescribed an exaggerated slim waist, nudes were also given such a slender waist, while, for instance, in the 1920s, when a straight and boyish silhouette prevailed in women's fashion, female nudes then failed to have a waist.

A body, moreover, is not static: it can move, it needs to be cared for and fed, it can adopt a pose and so on. Because people can express many things through their body, we have the notion of 'body language'.

Another point deserving attention is that jewellery is not worn constantly. A person having a substantial jewellery collection will wear most pieces every so often at best. The very act of taking off jewellery implies that one is at home again and ready, for instance, to go to bed. This moment may be charged erotically: in literature and films, the image of a woman removing her earrings is usually a metaphor of the ensuing sexual act, which as a

---

[3] Ted Polhemus, 'Text 1' in: *Les Fleurs du Mal*, ex. cat. MAK Österreichisches Museum für Angewandte Kunst, Vienna 2007, n.p.

Wie Menschen mit ihrem eigenen Körper umgehen und fremde Körper beurteilen, variiert mit dem Zeitgeist und von einer Kultur zur anderen. Vorstellungen vom nackten Körper werden häufig eher von Idealen bestimmt, die hinsichtlich der äußeren Schönheit in einer beliebigen Periode vorherrschen, als von einer anatomisch genauen Darstellung oder medizinisch verantwortungsvollen Behandlung des Körpers. Die Aktdarstellungen in der Geschichte der bildenden Kunst sind hierfür ein schönes Beispiel. In Zeiten, als die Mode eine übertrieben schmale Taille vorschrieb, wurden auch die Akte entsprechend schlank tailliert, während etwa in den 1920er-Jahren, als in der Damenmode eine gerade und knabenhafte Silhouette überwog, auch die weiblichen Akte keine Taillen hatten.

Darüber hinaus ist ein Körper nicht statisch: Er kann sich bewegen, muss gepflegt und ernährt werden, kann eine Pose annehmen und so weiter. Weil Menschen mit ihrem Körper viele Dinge ausdrücken können, kennen wir das Konzept der „Körpersprache".

Ein weiterer Punkt, der Beachtung verdient, ist die Tatsche, dass Schmuck nicht ständig getragen wird. Eine Person mit einer umfangreichen Schmucksammlung wird die meisten Stücke bestenfalls hin und wieder tragen. Das Ablegen von Schmuck signalisiert, dass man wieder zu Hause ist und beispielsweise bereit, ins Bett zu gehen. Dieser Moment kann erotisch aufgeladen sein: In Büchern und Filmen ist das Bild einer Frau, die ihre Ohrringe abnimmt, in der Regel eine Metapher für den anschließenden Liebesakt, was als Handlungselement meist dann interessant ist, wenn es sich auf ein erstes Mal oder einen Seitensprung bezieht.[4] Schmuck an- oder abzulegen, kann auch auf eine feierliche Funktion hindeuten, etwa bei religiösen Ornamenten oder Amtsketten, die nur in offiziellen beruflichen Zusammenhängen getragen werden.

Im Niederländischen trägt das Verb *versieren* (schmücken) eine Doppelbedeutung: Es steht auch für „jemanden verführen". Schmuckgegenstände eignen sich perfekt, um körperliche Reize hervorzuheben – in möglichen Varianten von zarter, kultivierter Erotik bis hin zu schamlosen, anzüglichen Ausdrucksformen. Viele Arten von Schmuck betonen eher das Gesicht, den Hals oder die Hände und Handgelenke als die primären Geschlechtsorgane. Auf jede erdenkliche Weise haben Männer ihre breiten Schultern mit aufwendigen Ketten herausgestellt. Der Busen, als sekundäres Geschlechtsmerkmal der Frau, nimmt einen wunderbaren Platz auf der Vorderseite des Körpers ein, direkt unterhalb des Gesichts und dicht am schlanken Hals – eine ideale Stelle, um Schmuck zu

---

4   Siehe unter anderem Len Deighton, *In Treu und Glauben. Roman einer Berliner Familie von 1899 bis 1945*, Bern/München/Wien 1988, S. 67–68.

plot element tends to be interesting when it refers to a first-timer or adultery.[4] Putting on or taking off jewellery may also be linked to a ceremonial function, such as religious ornaments and chains of office, which are worn in formal professional contexts only.

In Dutch the verb 'versieren' (to embellish) has a double meaning: it also means to seduce someone. Jewellery items are perfect for accentuating physical attractions. This may range from delicate, refined eroticism to flagrant, offensive expressions. Many kinds of jewellery will rather accentuate the face, the neck or the hands and the wrists rather than the primary sexual organs. In all sorts of ways men have accentuated their broad shoulders with elaborate chains. Breasts, as a secondary sexual feature of women, take up a wonderful spot on the front side of the body, right below the face and close to the slim neck: an ideal position for wearing jewellery. But this does not yet mean that necklaces for women always have an erotic effect. The interplay between jewellery and clothing, accessories, make-up, movement and posture provides the best indication of whether a piece of jewellery is meant to accentuate sexual attraction. A necklace with a pendant can be read as a sign of prudishness or frumpiness on one woman, while on another woman it may rather feature as a seductive element. The context in which a piece of jewellery is worn co-determines its effect, and this does not just apply to erotic effects.

Surely, there are instructive sides to the erotic dimension of jewellery for the theorist of jewellery as well as for the jewellery designer in search of inspiration. For one thing, eroticism has been studied from many different angles. Eroticism has also been represented in interesting ways, which proved useful for the study of the decorative aspects of jewellery. The careful study of nudes in painting, for example, has resulted in new information on jewellery items from the Renaissance or the first half of the twentieth century.[5] A nude, after all, as an object of desire is deemed to be even more erotic when still wearing a hat or shoes, or a few jewellery items.

Art is not a standard for quality

One of the art-historical issues that seem to recur in contemporary reflection on jewellery is the confusion that has emerged in the past decades about the notion of art in relation to jewellery, and in particular about how the notion of art was improperly elevated to a standard of quality in jewellery. It is undeniable that as of the 1960s the boundaries between the fine arts and the applied arts

---

4   See, among others, Len Deighton, *Winter. A Berlin Family, 1899–1945*, London 1987, pp. 63–64.
5   Evert Nijland, Pendants, Amsterdam 1997. Evert Nijland is an example of a young Dutch jewellery designer whose work has been clearly inspired by portraits, in particular by nudes from the Renaissance.

tragen. Das heißt jedoch noch nicht, dass Halsketten bei Frauen immer erotisch wirken müssen. Das Zusammenspiel zwischen Schmuck und Kleidung, Accessoires, Make-up, Bewegung und Haltung liefert den besten Hinweis darauf, ob ein Schmuckstück die sexuelle Anziehungskraft unterstreichen soll oder nicht. Eine Halskette mit Anhänger kann bei der einen Frau als Zeichen von Prüderie und Altbackenheit verstanden werden, bei der nächsten aber als verführerisches Element in Erscheinung treten. Nicht nur für erotische Effekte gilt: Der Kontext, in dem ein Schmuckstück getragen wird, bestimmt seine Wirkung mit.

Gewiss ist die erotische Dimension von Schmuck für die Schmucktheoretikerin oder den Schmucktheoretiker ebenso aufschlussreich wie für die Schmuckschaffenden auf der Suche nach Inspiration. Zum einen ist die Erotik aus zahlreichen unterschiedlichen Blickwinkeln untersucht worden. Zum anderen wurde sie auf vielfältige und interessante Weise dargestellt, was sich für die Betrachtung der dekorativen Aspekte von Schmuck als nützlich erwies. Das sorgfältige Studium von Akten in der Malerei zum Beispiel hat dazu geführt, dass moderne Schmuckgegenstände von neuen Einflüssen aus der Renaissance oder der ersten Hälfte des 20. Jahrhunderts geprägt werden.[5] Schließlich wird ein nackter Körper als Objekt der Begierde sogar für erotischer gehalten, wenn er noch einen Hut oder Schuhe oder etwas Schmuck trägt.

Kunst ist kein Qualitätsmaßstab

Einer der kunsthistorischen Streitpunkte, die gegenwärtig in der Schmuckbetrachtung wiederzukehren scheinen, betrifft die in den letzten Jahrzehnten aufgekommene Verwirrung über das Verhältnis von Kunst und Schmuck und insbesondere darüber, wie der Kunstbegriff unpassenderweise zum Qualitätsmaßstab für Schmuck erhoben wurde. Es ist unbestritten, dass die Grenzen zwischen der Bildenden Kunst und der Angewandten Kunst oder Gestaltung seit den 1960er-Jahren so erbittert infrage gestellt werden wie irgendeine Staatsgrenze auf dem Balkan. In Diskussionen aber, die darauf abzielen, die „besten" Arbeiten von Schmuckdesignern und anderen Gestaltern als Kunst zu deklarieren, wird das Kriterium der „Kunst" als Qualitätsmaßstab angewandt – was grundlegend falsch ist. Kunst ist kein Indiz für Qualität, sondern eine allgemeine Kategorie.

Aus meiner Sicht besitzt ein Schmuckstück genuine Qualität, wenn es die Kriterien des Umfassenden und der Präzision erfüllt – wenn es nicht nur gut gestaltet ist, sondern auch einen gewissen Symbolcharakter in Bezug auf eine

---

5 Evert Nijland, Pendants, Amsterdam 1997. Evert Nijland ist ein Beispiel für einen jungen niederländischen Schmuckdesigner, der sich in seiner Arbeit von Porträts inspirieren lässt, speziell von Aktdarstellungen aus der Renaissance.

or design have been challenged as fiercely as any state border in the Balkans. But in discussions geared to labelling the 'best' work of jewellery designers and other designers as art, the category of 'art' is deployed as a quality standard and this is fundamentally wrong. Art is not an indication of quality; it is a generic category.

In my opinion, a piece of jewellery has genuine quality when it meets the criteria of comprehensiveness and precision – when it not only is well designed but also embodies a measure of representativeness in relation to a society or cultural context. A piece of jewellery is valuable when it reflects a view on or a specific function of jewellery, thus offering wearers a base for linking their own identity and emotions to it. When one exclusively associates jewellery's supreme value with its artistic qualities and the use of precious materials, one is likely to ignore other values jewellery may comprise, like its social, historic and emotional values. Whether or not jewellery is conceived as one of the so-called autonomous arts is irrelevant; one should rather relate it to all the various nice and not so nice qualities that define us as human beings. The power of jewellery is that it reaches way beyond any work of fine art, simply because jewellery always involves a human dimension. Jewellery has a social, physical and emotional complexity which is rarely addressed from an art-historical angle. Worn by somebody, a piece of jewellery will leave the house – and it will be seen in all sorts of places and venues.

In the current era, marked by political and economic instability as well as energy scarcity and ideological confusion about social norms and values, incentives for new developments may come from all directions, from the most intimate thoughts of individual makers to more or less organised grassroots protests within subcultures. And equally from designers with a fine sensibility for fashion and cultural developments who put their talents at the service of commercial pursuits. To be honest, within our capitalist society the latter seem quite eligible to be considered as model representatives of their day and age, particularly when also taking into account the prominence and massive scale of modern production and communication technologies.

It is in this configuration that the contribution of individual jewellery designers has its merits for their profession. How do they deal with the conventions in their discipline? In which ways do they address jewellery as a means for marking an identity? Today one will see many references, ironical or not, to the traditional cornerstones of the jewellery discipline. To invoke the concept of fine art as the only standard of quality is fundamentally misguided.

To my opinion, there is no reason to worry about the future of jewellery. Jewellery is a primordial phenomenon, and it is so dear and near to human

Gesellschaft oder einen kulturellen Kontext verkörpert. Ein Schmuckstück ist wertvoll, wenn es einen Standpunkt zum Medium Schmuck oder eine spezielle Funktion von Schmuck reflektiert und so den Trägern eine Basis bietet, um ihre eigene Identität und Gefühlswelt mit ihm in Verbindung zu bringen. Knüpft man den höchsten Wert von Schmuck ausschließlich an seine künstlerischen Eigenschaften und die Verwendung edler Materialien, dann läuft man Gefahr, andere in ihm enthaltene Werte, etwa gesellschaftlicher, historischer oder emotionaler Natur, zu übersehen. Ob man Schmuck als eine der sogenannten eigenständigen Künste begreift oder nicht, ist irrelevant; man sollte ihn vielmehr mit den vielen schönen und weniger schönen Eigenschaften in Zusammenhang bringen, die uns als Menschen ausmachen. Die Macht des Schmucks besteht darin, dass er weit über jedes Werk der bildenden Kunst hinausreicht, eben weil er immer auch eine menschliche Dimension umfasst. Schmuck besitzt eine soziale, physische und emotionale Vielschichtigkeit, die aus kunsthistorischer Perspektive selten thematisiert wird. Wird ein Schmuckstück von jemandem getragen, verlässt es früher oder später das Haus – und wird an allen möglichen Orten und Schauplätzen gesehen.

In der heutigen Zeit, die von politischer und wirtschaftlicher Instabilität ebenso gekennzeichnet ist wie von Energieknappheit und ideologischer Verwirrung über gesellschaftliche Normen und Werte, können Anreize für neue Entwicklungen aus allen Richtungen kommen, von den intimsten Gedanken einzelner Macher bis zu mehr oder weniger organisierten Basisprotesten innerhalb von Subkulturen – und genauso gut von Designern mit einem feinen Gespür für Mode und kulturelle Entwicklungen, die ihre Talente in den Dienst gewerblicher Betätigung stellen. Ehrlich gesagt erscheinen Letztere in unserer kapitalistischen Gesellschaft durchaus geeignet, um als mustergültige Repräsentanten ihrer Zeit zu gelten – vor allem, wenn man auch die Bedeutung und das gewaltige Ausmaß der modernen Produktions- und Kommunikationstechnologien berücksichtigt.

In eben dieser Konstellation leisten individuelle Schmuckdesigner verdienstvolle Beiträge für ihren Berufsstand. Wie gehen sie mit den Konventionen in ihrem Fach um? Inwiefern behandeln sie Schmuck als Mittel, um eine Identität kenntlich zu machen? Ob ironisch oder nicht, heute sind zahlreiche Bezüge zu den traditionellen Eckpfeilern des Mediums Schmuck erkennbar. Sich auf den Begriff der Bildenden Kunst als einzigen Qualitätsmaßstab zu berufen, ist von Grund auf unangebracht.

Nach meinem Dafürhalten besteht kein Anlass, sich um die Zukunft des Schmucks zu sorgen. Schmuck ist ein Urphänomen und den Menschen mit all ihren Eigenarten so lieb und teuer, dass er jede zeitübergreifende Entwicklung

beings and all their idiosyncrasies that it will survive each and every development or fluctuation across time. Somehow, it will always be reflective of its own day and age. In all eras people have let themselves be tempted by wearable ornaments, by their shapes, materials, techniques and symbolism, also in times of war and disaster. But the question of whether jewellery can make a person happy will almost always be denounced as proof of vanity or of a penchant for luxury. The automatic answer is denial: other things will make people feel happy. This, too, is a prejudice that needs to be eliminated.

In essence, jewellery is a catalyst of desires and fears, of emotions, sexual energy, social relationships and the need for identity – of everything, in short, that drives and excites people in their day-to-day lives. If we are aware of the huge number of decorative and symbolic values embodied by jewellery across its prolonged history and of the elementary motivations underlying the wearing of jewellery, we will always be able to find an affirmation of our identity and desires in these tiny objects on the basis of reciprocity – and hence we will find something that makes us happy. Within a multidisciplinary approach towards jewellery, it is safe to argue that even those who feel most at ease when not wearing jewellery and who even refuse to contemplate jewellery still present an interesting case for further thinking on jewellery, because they will be wearing some sort of adornment anyway, whether it is a watch, a logo or a specific pair of shoes.

This text presents a compilation of ideas from *Sieraad in context. Een multidisciplinair kader voor de beschouwing van het sieraad* (Jewellery in context. A multidisciplinary framework for reflection on jewellery), dissertation, Leiden University, 2010.

oder Schwankung überstehen wird. Irgendwie wird er stets seine eigene Zeit widerspiegeln. In allen Epochen, selbst in Kriegs- und Katastrophenzeiten, haben sich Menschen von tragbaren Ornamenten verführen lassen, ihren Formen, Materialien, Techniken und ihrer Symbolik. Die Frage aber, ob Schmuck einen Menschen glücklich machen kann, wird fast ausnahmslos als Beweis für Eitelkeit oder Hang zum Luxus verurteilt. Die automatische Antwort besteht im Leugnen: es sind andere Dinge, die Menschen glücklich machen. Auch dieses Vorurteil gilt es auszuräumen.

Im Wesentlichen ist Schmuck ein Katalysator für Begierden und Ängste, für Gefühle, sexuelle Energie, soziale Beziehungen und das Bedürfnis nach Identität – kurzum für alles, was Menschen in ihrem Alltag antreibt und begeistert. Solange wir uns der Vielzahl an dekorativen und symbolischen Werten, die der Schmuck in seiner ausgedehnten Geschichte verkörpert hat, und der grundlegenden Motivationen bewusst sind, die dem Tragen von Schmuck zugrunde liegen, werden wir stets imstande sein, in diesen winzigen Objekten nach dem Prinzip der Gegenseitigkeit eine Bestätigung unserer Identität und unserer Sehnsüchte zu entdecken – und somit etwas finden, das uns glücklich macht. Im Rahmen einer multidisziplinären Annäherung an das Medium Schmuck kann man mit Sicherheit argumentieren, dass selbst Menschen, die sich am wohlsten fühlen, wenn sie keinen Schmuck tragen, und die sich sogar weigern, Schmuck überhaupt in Erwägung zu ziehen, dennoch interessante Fälle für ein weiteres Nachdenken über Schmuck abgeben – denn irgendeine Art von Verzierung werden sie in jedem Fall tragen, sei es eine Uhr, ein Logo oder ein bestimmtes Paar Schuhe.

Dieser Text präsentiert gesammelte Gedanken aus der Dissertation *Sieraad in context. Een multidiciplinair kader voor de beschouwing van het sieraad* (Schmuck im Kontext. Ein multidisziplinärer Rahmen für die Betrachtung von Schmuck), Universität Leiden, 2010.

reMake

Schmuck im Museum

Julia Wild

Ein Museum ist ein Ort, an dem Dinge, Artefakte, Kunst archiviert, wissenschaftlich aufgearbeitet und in Beziehung zum Betrachtenden gestellt werden. Es wird ein Dialog zwischen Besucherin oder Besucher und dem Objekt initiiert, der über das Individuum hinausgeht und übergeordnete gesellschaftliche Fragen aufwirft. Ein Museum, insbesondere ein städtisches Museum, wie es das Simeonstift in Trier ist, trägt dazu bei, die Identität eines Ortes und ihrer Bewohner zu definieren.

     Museen sind gesellschaftliche Institutionen, die kulturhistorisch betrachtet relativ jung sind, deren Anfänge in der Aufklärung lagen und die erst im Laufe des 19. Jahrhunderts an Bedeutung gewannen. Die Schmuckabteilungen vieler Museen – wie beispielsweise das Victoria & Albert Museum in London oder das Rijksmuseum in Amsterdam – erfreuen sich großer Beliebtheit beim Publikum. Ist es allein das Strahlen der Diamanten und die verwendeten, kostbaren Materialien, welche die Menschen so magisch anziehen? Sicherlich spielt die Materialität eine wichtige Rolle, doch genauso entscheidend ist der Objektcharakter des Schmucks, in dem sich die Materialität erst ausdrückt und erlebbar wird. Denn die wenigsten Menschen schauen ebenso fasziniert auf die Porträts hochgestellter Personen, die uns so zahlreich von den Wänden der Museen dieser Welt anblicken. Auch dort wäre Schmuck in reicher Auswahl und zudem in seiner Funktion zu bewundern. Aber im Bild verliert der Schmuck seinen Objektcharakter, die Idee des Haptischen, die in der musealen Auslage zu erahnen ist, auch wenn der Schmuck hinter Glas verschlossen liegt. Das zweidimensionale Bild eröffnet zwar eine Tragesituation, aber erst in der Präsentation als Objekt im Museum können sich die Betrachtenden das Schmuckstück in ihrer Vorstellung aneignen, sich hineinversetzen. Damit schafft das Museum eine Situation, in der die ausgestellte Arbeit die Wahrnehmung anregt und im besten Falle emotional berührt.

     Das Projekt „re*Make*" der Hochschule Trier in Zusammenarbeit mit dem Simeonstift ermöglichte es den Studierenden der Fachrichtung Edelstein und Schmuck, sowohl den musealen Raum und seine Funktionen als auch ihr Schmuckschaffen zu reflektieren und in Beziehung zueinander zu stellen. Inspiriert vom Museum als Ort und den darin ausgestellten Objekten entstanden Schmuckstücke und Installationen, die ein Ausdruck für die Wirkung sind, die ein solcher Ort der Erinnerung hervorrufen kann. Es war ein mehrstufiger Dialog, der hier angestoßen werden sollte: Die Studierenden reagierten mit ihren Arbeiten auf die Stücke des Museums, welche dann gemeinsam ausgestellt wurden, um wiederum Besucherinnen und Besucher dazu anzuregen, diese mit einem neuen Blick zu betrachten.

Jewellery in a Museum

Julia Wild

A museum is a place in which things, artefacts and art are archived, subjected to scholarly treatment and related to the viewer. A dialogue is initiated between the object and visitors to the museum. This dialogue goes beyond the individual and raises overriding social questions. A museum, particularly a municipal museum, which is what the City Museum Simeonstift in Trier is, contributes to defining the identity of a place and its inhabitants.

Museums are social institutions which, viewed from the standpoint of cultural history, are relatively recent. Although their beginnings lie in the Age of Enlightenment, they only gained in importance over the course of the nineteenth century. The jewellery departments of many museums – such as, for example, the Victoria & Albert Museum in London and the Rijksmuseum in Amsterdam – are very popular with the public. Is it just the sparkle of the diamonds and the precious, costly materials used in jewellery making that draw people as if by magic? The material aspect is bound to play an important role, yet the object character of jewellery, in which the material used for it is first expressed and is experienceable in the jewellery, is just as crucial. After all, very few people are equally fascinated when glancing at the portraits of high-ranking persons that stare down at us in such numbers from the walls of the world's museums. There, too, a wide range of jewellery might be admired and, what is more, in its functional context. But in a picture, jewellery loses its object character, the idea of tactility, hints of which are given in museum displays even though the jewellery remains closed off behind glass. The two-dimensional picture does open up a wearing situation, but viewers can only appropriate the piece of jewellery in their ideas of it, empathise with it, when it is presented as an object in a museum. Thus a museum creates a situation in which a work displayed stimulates viewers' perceptions and, in the best case, appeals to their emotion by moving them.

The Trier University of Applied Sciences re*Make* project jointly with the Simeonstift enabled students from the Department of Gemstones and Jewellery to reflect on the museum space and its function as well as the jewellery they were making and to relate them to each other. Inspired by the museum as a place and the objects displayed in it, pieces of jewellery and installations were made that express the impact a place of memory like this can have. It represented a dialogue on several levels that is to be touched on here: students reacted with their work to pieces in the museum, which were then exhibited alongside the works that inspired them in order to stimulate visitors to view the museum objects with different eyes.

Warum ist ein Museum – zumal ein stadthistorisches Museum – geeignet für ein solches Projekt mit Studierenden, die sich mit Schmuck und Edelsteinen beschäftigen? Es ist zunächst die Institution, unabhängig von der thematischen Ausrichtung, die eine Anbindung an den Schmuck auch auf theoretischer Ebene interessant macht. In der kunsthistorischen Forschung wird vom Museum als rituellem Ort gesprochen, an dem sich Menschen und ausgestellte Objekte in einem außeralltäglichen Rahmen begegnen. So verweist in der Regel bereits die Architektur auf die Besonderheit des Ortes. Wenn das Museum nicht wie in Trier bereits in einem ehemaligen sakralen und repräsentativen Bau Aufnahme gefunden hat, orientierte sich die Museumsarchitektur der letzten beiden Jahrhunderte häufig an Tempelanlagen. Imposante Vorbauten und repräsentative, hallenartige Eingangsbereiche schaffen eine Situation, die einen klaren Bruch zur Welt außerhalb des Museums herstellen und ein Innehalten hervorrufen soll. Indem die Besucherin oder der Besucher aus dem Alltag heraustritt, verändert sich die Wahrnehmung der Ausstellungsstücke. Sie sind keine Gebrauchsgegenstände mehr, sondern Dinge, die zur Reflexion anregen, wobei die Museumsleitung den Objekten durch Kontextualisierung einen Sinn zuschreibt. Die Betrachtenden erfahren diesen durch die Beschreibung der beigestellten Texte und mittels des Dialogs der zur Ausstellung gehörenden Dinge. Darüber hinaus stellt das Objekt einen sinnlichen Mehrwert bereit, welcher Erinnerungen, Assoziationen hervorruft, die oftmals weder von den Kuratierenden noch dem Publikum steuerbar sind.

Das Museum und seine Atmosphäre des Außeralltäglichen machen es möglich, dass diese Aura der Dinge wahrgenommen, erfahrbar gemacht wird. Man tritt aus dem Zeitfluss des Alltags heraus, hält inne und ist im Moment der Betrachtung eines Objekts im besonderen Maße präsent. Gerade ein historisches Museum unterliegt einer narrativen Struktur, indem es Vergangenes aus den Archiven hervorholt, dem Vergessen entreißt, in das Jetzt überführt und Künftiges durch die Vergegenwärtigung beeinflusst. Damit formt ein Museum die Identität der Besucherinnen und Besucher sowie der Bewohnerinnen und Bewohner des Ortes, auf den sich das Museum bezieht. Aber auch die von weiter entfernt Anreisenden werden durch den Anblick eines bestimmten Objekts an etwas erinnert. Durch die Betrachtung kann etwas bewusst gemacht werden, das unter Umständen das Bild vom eigenen Selbst verändern kann.

In einem Museum stehen der Ausstellungsraum, der Mensch und die Objekte in einer Wechselwirkung und ermöglichen ein Erleben sowohl auf intellektueller als auch emotionaler Ebene. Die Wirkung des Schmucks entfaltet sich in der Beziehung zwischen der Person, die den Schmuck für sich auswählt und trägt, denjenigen, die die Geschmückten betrachten und – insbesondere im zeitgenössischen Schmuck – den Schmuckschaffenden. Da Schmuck im rituellen Handeln

Why is a museum – especially a municipal history museum – suitable for a project of this kind with students who study jewellery and gemstones? First of all, it is the institution, regardless of its thematic orientation, that makes linkage with jewellery interesting on the theoretical plane as well. Art-historical scholarship speaks of museums as ritual places where visitors and the objects on display can meet in a setting that is supramundane. Even museum architecture as a rule alludes to the exceptional status of the museum as a site. When a museum is not already housed, as it is in Trier, in a grand, formerly sacred building, museum architecture has in the past two centuries often been inspired by temple precincts. Impressive porches and showy, hall-like entrance areas create a situation that is intended to clearly demarcate the outside world from the museum itself and compel visitors to stop and recollect themselves before entering. Because they are stepping out of their mundane everyday existence when they enter a museum, visitors' perception of the exhibits inside changes. They are now things that inspire reflection and no longer utilitarian objects. The head of the museum ascribes a meaning to the objects by contextualising them. Viewers experience them via the descriptions in the label texts and the dialogue with the things that belong to the exhibition. Moreover, the object provides a sensory added value which elicits in visitors memories and associations that often elude the guidance of curators and viewers alike.

The museum and its exceptional atmosphere make it possible for this aura of the things in it to be perceived and experienced. One steps outside the everyday flow of time, stops to reflect and is consciously present to an exceptional degree when viewing an object. History museums in particular are underpinned by a narrative structure because they bring the past out from the archives, wresting it from oblivion to transfer it to the present and bringing influence to bear on the future by visualisation. Thus a museum – especially a municipal museum – shapes the identities of visitors and residents of the place that is the museum catchment area. However, the sight of a given object can remind even visitors from further away of something. Viewing can make one aware of something that in some circumstances can change the way one sees oneself.

In a museum, the exhibition space, visitors and objects interrelate and this makes experiencing possible on both the intellectual and emotional planes. The impact jewellery makes develops in the relationship between the persons who have chosen the jewellery for themselves and wear it, those who look at the person wearing the jewellery and – especially where contemporary jewellery is concerned – the person who has made the jewellery. Since jewellery has always played a role in ritual observances, the behavioural mechanisms asso-

des Menschen immer eine Rolle gespielt hat, sind die Wirkmechanismen der Schmuck- und Museumserfahrung in vielem ähnlich und machen ein solches Projekt so interessant. Denn auch im Schmuck geht es um Außeralltäglichkeit, um Präsenz, die Bewusstwerdung des Moments im zeitlichen Ablauf der Historie. Es geht um die Konstruktion von Identität, wie sie durch das Tragen von Schmuck gestaltet und vermittelt werden kann.

Schmuck gilt als die älteste überlieferte symbolische Ausdrucksform des Menschen. Die Gründe, Schmuck zu tragen und die Art und Weise, wie Schmuck wahrgenommen wird, sind im Laufe der Jahrtausende und über die Vielzahl der Kulturen hinweg gleich geblieben. Nur die Bedeutungsschwerpunkte und die Interpretation der Zeichen, die Schmuck beinhalten kann, unterliegen innerhalb eines festgeschriebenen Rahmens einem historisch-kulturellen Wandel. Der Wunsch sich zu schmücken, lässt sich auf verschiedene Gründe zurückführen: zunächst auf das Bedürfnis, sein Äußeres zu verändern, sich zu verschönern und zu schmücken – zweckfrei, spielerisch, schon bei Kindern beobachtbar. Ein weiteres Motiv liegt in dem Wunsch begründet, ein Zeichen zu besitzen und zu tragen, welches Trägerin oder Träger an einen besonderen Menschen oder einen bedeutsamen Ort erinnert. Es kann aber auch die Erinnerung an einen speziellen Moment im Leben – den eines Abschieds oder Neubeginns – gegenwärtig halten. Schmuck als Träger von Erinnerung stellt den bei weitem wichtigsten Aspekt von Schmuck in der heutigen Zeit dar. Diese Erinnerungsfunktion entfaltet ihre Wirkung vor allem nach innen, weniger nach außen: die Betrachtenden können nicht wissen, dass die Halskette der Großmutter gehörte oder von der ersten Reise nach Asien stammt. Nur die Trägerin oder der Träger weiß um die Bedeutung des Schmuckstückes. Es gibt zwar Schmuck, der an etwas erinnert und von Außenstehenden in einem gewissen Rahmen lesbar ist wie zum Beispiel der Ehering oder die Ehrennadel. Aber die vollständige Dimension der Erinnerung an die Situation, in der der Schmuck eine besondere Rolle spielte und weshalb er im Jetzt an das Vergangene erinnern kann, ist nur für die Trägerin oder den Träger zugänglich. Darüber hinaus kann das Schmuckobjekt als Kristallisationspunkt von Erzählungen zu einem konstitutiven Element von Gemeinschaft werden. In Gesellschaften, deren Traditionen auf mündlicher Überlieferung beruhen, ist Schmuck häufig Ausgangspunkt für gemeinschaftsstiftende Erzählungen und Erinnerungen. Aber auch in unserer Gesellschaft, in der die Kleinfamilie oder der Freundeskreis das soziale Miteinander prägen, kann der Schmuck und die daran haftende Erinnerung zu einem wichtigen Erzählkern der Gemeinschaft werden.

Die Suche nach Schutz, der sich in den Schmuckformen der Amulette und Talismane ausdrücken kann, ist ein weiterer Beweggrund, sich zu schmücken. Dieser Schmuck hat die Funktion, vor Unheil in der realen Welt – Krankheiten, Feinden und gefährlichen Tieren –, aber auch vor immateriellen Gefahren wie Geistern und

ciated with experiencing jewellery and a museum are similar in many respects and are what make a project of this kind so interesting. After all, jewellery, too, is all about the supramundane, about presence, about becoming aware of the moment in the temporal course of history. What is at stake here is the construction of identity, as it can be designed and conveyed by wearing jewellery.

Jewellery is regarded as man's most ancient symbolic form of expression that has come down to us. The reasons for choosing jewellery for oneself and wearing it and the way in which jewellery is perceived by observers have remained the same over thousands of years in a great many civilisations. Only the semantic focus and the interpretation of the signs that jewellery can contain are subject to historical and cultural change within an established paradigm. Thus the various reasons for human beings' desire to adorn themselves can be traced: first, the need to change their appearance, to make themselves more beautiful, to adorn themselves in the conventional sense – without a purpose, playfully, as can already be observed in children. Another motive is grounded in the desire to possess and wear a badge reminding the wearer of a special person or a place that has been significant for him or her. It can, however, also keep the memory of a special moment in the wearer's life – a farewell or a fresh start – alive. Being the vehicle for memory represents by far the most important aspect of jewellery in today's world. This mnemonic function develops its impact above all internally, less so externally: viewers cannot know that the necklace belonged to the wearer's grandmother or was brought back from the wearer's first trip to Asia. Only the wearer knows the true meaning of the piece of jewellery s/he is wearing. Wedding rings and badges of honour, on the other hand, are jewellery that is a remembrance of something and is, within a specific framework, legible for viewers as well. Nonetheless, only the wearer has access to the complete range of memories of the situation in which a given piece of jewellery has played a special role and to why it can recall the past in the here and now. For others the jewellery object can become a constitutive element of community by virtue of being a focal point of narratives. In societies with traditions based on oral transmission, jewellery is often the starting point for communitarian narratives and recollections. In our society, too, in which the nuclear family or one's circle of friends shape social life, jewellery and the memories associated with it can become an important communal narrative core.

The quest for protection that may be expressed in such forms of jewellery as amulets and talismans is another motive for adorning oneself. Such jewellery has the function of protecting the wearer from the evils of the real world – disease, enemies and dangerous animals – as well as from dangers that are incorporeal, such as evil spirits and curses. The wearer of specific jewellery can

Flüchen zu beschützen. Durch das Tragen eines bestimmten Schmucks kann man sich ermächtigt fühlen, Situationen und Probleme zu bewältigen. Meist haben diese Schmuckstücke auch einen Erinnerungsaspekt. Denn indem sie an Vergangenes, an positive Erlebnisse oder bestimmte Personen erinnern, fühlen sich Trägerin oder Träger in der aktuellen Situation gestärkt. Hier erkennt man, dass es kaum möglich ist, eine scharfe Trennlinie zwischen den unterschiedlichen Funktionen des Schmucktragens zu ziehen und sie sich wechselseitig beeinflussen können bzw. je nach Situation unterschiedlich wahrgenommen werden.

Schmuck dient nicht zuletzt als Statussymbol. Er bezeichnet den gesellschaftlichen Stand der Geschmückten, ihre Position in der Gemeinschaft, die von dieser anerkannt werden muss, indem sie das getragene Zeichen akzeptiert. Schmuck in diesem Sinn ist in einem komplexen sozialen Zeichensystem eingebettet, welches der gesellschaftlichen Kontrolle unterliegt und auf ein Ordnungssystem verweist. In diesem Kontext möchte ich auf die Schmuckform Krone eingehen, um zu zeigen wie sich die Funktion eines Schmuckobjektes innerhalb unserer Kultur verändert hat: die Krone zeichnete im europäischen Mittelalter die Tragenden als Angehörige eines gesellschaftlichen Standes aus und definierte ihre Rolle innerhalb einer Gemeinschaft. Die Krone verwies zwar auch – aufgrund der kostbaren Materialien, die verarbeitet wurden – auf zur Schau getragenen Wohlstand, doch die eigentliche Bedeutung lag in ihrem Zeichencharakter, der einen Herrschaftsanspruches verdeutlichte und über das Bildprogramm der Krone auf einen metaphysischen Rahmen verwies. Trägerin und Träger der Krone waren nicht nur Repräsentanten einer Gemeinschaft, sondern verstanden sich auch in der Tradition und Nachfolge der biblischen Könige und des Weltenherrschers Christi stehend. Als solches musste das erstmalige Anlegen sowie das Geschmücktsein mit der Krone in besonderen Festakten, welche die Herrschaft und die soziale Rolle der Gekrönten bestätigten, von der Gemeinschaft in einem rituellen Rahmen anerkannt werden. In der Vormoderne wäre es daher nicht möglich gewesen, sich für das Tragen einer Krone aus rein ästhetischen Gründen zu entscheiden. Nicht finanzielle Mittel bestimmten die Entscheidung, welcher Schmuck von einer Person getragen werden durfte, sondern allein ihr Stand innerhalb der Gesellschaft. Zahlreiche Kleider- und Schmuckverordnungen des Mittelalters und der frühen Neuzeit zeugen von diesem Ordnungsverständnis.

Noch immer gibt es in einigen europäischen Ländern die traditionelle Krönung eines Herrschers nach genau festgelegten Zeremonien. Diese haben aber keine politische Bedeutung mehr, da das Königtum in Europa nur noch eine repräsentative Funktion besitzt. Die Krone ist nicht mehr Herrschaftszeichen, sondern symbolischer Bezugspunkt einer Nation. Die Krone ist nicht mehr Bindeglied einer auf persönlichen Beziehungen beruhenden Gemeinschaft, die wechselseitig von

feel empowered to deal with situations and problems. These pieces of jewellery usually also have a commemorative aspect. Because these pieces remind wearers of the past, positive experiences or particular persons, they feel affirmation in any given situation. Here one realises that distinguishing definitively between the various functions of wearing jewellery is impossible and accepts the fact that they can influence each other or be perceived differently with each different situation.

Last but not least, jewellery serves as a status symbol. It designates the wearer's social rank, his or her position in society, which society must recognise by accepting the sign as worn. Jewellery in this sense is embedded in a complex social system of signs which is subject to societal control and refers to a system of ordering. In this context I should like to go into the crown as a form of jewellery in order to show how the function of a jewellery object has changed within our culture even though it has not lost its meaning as a status symbol: In medieval Europe, the crown designated its wearer as a member of a social class and defined his role within a community. The crown also alluded – on the basis of the precious materials used to make it – to the wearer's wealth, yet its actual meaning lay in its symbolic character, which clarified claims to absolute power, divinely conferred, and referred above and beyond the iconographic programme of the crown to a metaphysical frame of reference. The wearer of the crown was not only a representative of a community but also saw him- or herself as participating in the tradition and the succession of the biblical kings and of Christ, Lord of the World. The wearer's coronation and adornment with the crown on special festive occasions affirming the power and social role of the person crowned were accepted as such by the community in a ritual framework. Hence it would not have been possible in the early modern age to opt for wearing a crown for purely aesthetic reasons. Nor was it the financial means available to a person that determined the decision about what jewellery might be worn; it was solely that person's social status. Numerous sumptuary laws governing the wearing of clothing and jewellery in the Middle Ages and the early modern age attest to this interpretation of order, aimed principally at the rising mercantile class that was outside the established order of the estates yet also attained via jewellery a symbolic place in society.

In some European countries there are still monarchies, and the traditional coronation of a king or queen takes place according to precisely prescribed ceremonies. They no longer have any political significance, however, because the monarchy in Europe now possesses only ceremonial functions. The crown is no longer a symbol of power but rather the symbolic point of reference for a nation. The crown is no longer a link in a community based on personal relationships

den während der Krönungszeremonie anwesenden Adeligen und dem gekrönten Herrscher bestätigt wird, sondern ist materielles, strahlendes Zeichen der Geschichte und Identität einer Gemeinschaft. Die Krone ist weiterhin das Erkennungszeichen des gesellschaftlichen Standes der Gekrönten, darüber hinaus verweist das Material der Krone auf die Reichtümer eines Königshauses, aber in erster Linie hat sich die Bedeutung und der Grund des Schmückens in Richtung der einigenden, repräsentativen Funktion dieses besonderen Schmucks verschoben. Sie bewegt sich noch im Bezugsfeld eines Statussymbols, aber die Wahrnehmung und die Interpretation des Zeichens Krone hat sich im Lauf der Zeit verändert.

Wie sehr die Bedeutung der Verwendung eines Schmuckstücks vom Kontext abhängig ist, kann man daran erkennen, wie unsere heutige Gesellschaft auf jemanden reagieren würde, der mit einer Krone geschmückt in einem Cabrio durch Beverly Hills führe, in einen öffentlichen Bus steigen oder auf einer privaten Abendveranstaltung erscheinen würde, die Krone als Teil eines Bühnenauftritts verwenden oder sie in einer Vitrine in einem Privatmuseum ausstellen würde. Die Beispiele sollen deutlich machen, dass die Auswahl des Schmucks – ob Krone oder einfache Halskette – und die damit einhergehenden Intentionen des Schmückens jedem selbst überlassen bleibt und von den Betrachterinnen und Betrachtern jeweils nach dem Kontext des Schmückens bewertet, aber nicht sanktioniert wird. Unabhängig für welche Auftrittssituation man sich entscheiden würde, im Falle des Schmückens mit einer Krone hätte es immer etwas mit Status zu tun, doch in einem anderen Sinn als in der Vormoderne: in diesen hypothetischen Situationen würden wir als Publikum der Situation nicht die Rolle einnehmen, die in vergangenen Zeiten Adelige innehatten, nämlich die der bestätigenden Zeuginnen und Zeugen eines Rituals, welches sowohl den Betrachteten als auch die Betrachtenden in ihren gesellschaftlichen Rollen festlegt, sondern wir wären passive Zuschauerinnen und Zuschauer unterschiedlicher Formen der Selbstdarstellung. Wir könnten uns über die Exzentrik der Situation amüsieren oder unbeteiligt wegschauen. Das Ereignis böte die Möglichkeit eines Small Talks mit dem linker Hand stehenden unbekannten Gast der bis dahin doch eher langweiligen Cocktailparty, oder es könnte Anlass für ein gebildetes Gespräch über die gestalterische Umsetzung der Krone und ihre gelungene oder eher doch nicht so gelungene Kontextualisierung sein.

Das Beispiel des Schmuckobjekts Krone soll zeigen, wie sich innerhalb des Bezugsfelds Statussymbol der soziale Handlungsrahmen und die Interpretation der verwendeten Zeichen verändern kann. So ist in unserer heutigen Gesellschaft die Darstellung des Selbst und nicht die Darstellung einer transzendenten Ordnung die vorherrschende Funktion des Schmucks. Für die Selbstdarstellung bräuchte es keine Betrachterinnen und Betrachter – auch in den eigenen vier Wänden könnte man sich mit einer Krone schmücken und daraus seine Freude

that is mutually affirmed by the nobility present during the coronation ceremony and the crowned monarch. Instead the crown is a material, albeit radiant, sign of the history and identity, of, for instance, the British nation. The crown continues to be the sign for recognising the social estate of the crowned. Moreover, the material of which the crown is made alludes to the riches of the British royal family. However, the significance of and the reason for adornment with this particular jewellery has shifted primarily towards its unifying, representative function. It is still within the referential field of a status symbol, but over the course of time the perception and interpretation of the crown as a sign have changed.

One can appreciate how much the meaning of the use to which a piece of jewellery is put is context-dependent when one considers how today's society would react to someone adorned with a real crown driving through Beverly Hills in a convertible, stepping onto a public bus, or appearing at a private evening party, using the crown as a stage prop, or putting it on show in a display case at a private museum. The examples enumerated are supposed to make clear that the choice of jewellery – be it a crown or a simple necklace – and the concomitant intentions of adorning oneself remain up to the individual and will be evaluated by observers depending on the given context of the act of adornment yet will not be disapproved of. Regardless of the performance context one might opt for, in the case of adorning oneself with a crown it would invariably have something to do with status, yet in a sense that differs from the significance attached to this act in early modern Europe: in these hypothetical situations we as observers of the situation would not assume the role played by nobles in the past – that is, as affirmative actors in a ritual which defines them and those who behold them in their societal roles. Instead we would be passive onlookers watching various different forms of self-representation. We might be amused at the oddness of the situation or, alternatively, look away because we are indifferent to it. The event would provide opportunity for small talk with an unknown guest standing to our left at a drinks party that had been dull up to then or it might provide a pretext for an erudite conversation on how the crown has been translated into design and whether its contextualisation has been successful or not so successful after all.

The example of the crown as a jewellery object is intended to demonstrate how the societal action space and the interpretation of the symbols used can change within the referential field that is a status symbol. For instance, the primary function of jewellery in today's society is representing the self rather than standing for a transcendent order. No viewer is needed for self-representation – one might adorn oneself with a crown, even within the four walls of one's

ziehen. Doch auch wenn die Art des Schmückens auf eigenen Entscheidungen beruht, sich vornehmlich auf das Selbst bezieht, möchte es in der Regel auch etwas nach außen kommunizieren, darstellen. So kann Schmuck sowohl auf den materiellen als auch immateriellen Hintergrund der Tragenden verweisen, beispielsweise auf deren Bildung und den von der Herkunft geprägten Geschmack. Der Wunsch, das eigene Bild seiner Selbst zu kommunizieren und nach außen zu tragen lässt Trägerinnen und Träger auch weiterhin auf die Wahrnehmung und Bewertung durch die Betrachtenden angewiesen sein. Nur durch die Reziprozität entfaltet der Schmuck seine volle soziale Wirkung. So ist die Bedeutung des Schmucks als Statussymbol auch heute noch vorhanden, aber der Fokus liegt stärker auf dem Selbst, dem Individuum, welches sich für den Schmuck entscheidet.

Das Motiv der Selbstdarstellung führt unmittelbar zu dem für die heutige Zeit so wichtigen Grund, sich zu schmücken: die Suche nach der eigenen Identität bzw. der Wunsch, die eigene Identität mit Hilfe äußerer Zeichen zu gestalten und zu festigen. Als ein Bereich des Schmucks ist hier insbesondere der sogenannte zeitgenössische Schmuck oder Autorenschmuck zu nennen. In diesem spielen die Schmuckschaffenden eine besondere Rolle, indem sie ihre Geschichte, ihre Identität aber auch ihr Erleben und Wahrnehmen des Zeitgeistes in die Gestaltung der Schmuckwerke einfließen lassen. Dadurch beziehen sich die Schmuckstücke eindeutig auf die, die sie geschaffen haben, aber sind in ihrer Zeichenhaftigkeit bestenfalls noch so mehrdeutig, dass sie für die Trägerin oder den Träger die Möglichkeit darstellen, den Ausdruck des eigenen Selbst durch das Schmuckstück zu ergänzen. Betrachterinnen und Betrachter hingegen werden dazu angeregt, das Schmuckstück einerseits in seiner Singularität wahrzunehmen, andererseits in Bezug zu dem Träger zu stellen. Was im Museum der Raum ist, der eine atmosphärische Betrachtungssituation der Dinge herstellt und zur Reflexion anregt, ist im Falle des Schmucks die Trägerin oder der Träger, die dem Schmuckstück eine Plattform geben, seine Aura zu entfalten, indem sich verschiedene Identitäten, die des Tragenden, des Betrachtenden und des Schmuckschaffenden, in dem Moment des Geschmücktseins miteinander verbinden.

Die Erfahrung eines Museumsbesuchs und die Gründe, Schmuck zu tragen, scheinen vordergründig weit auseinanderzuliegen. Doch in beiden Fällen steht der menschliche Umgang mit Objekten im Vordergrund. Die Wechselwirkung zwischen Mensch und Objekt lässt etwas Neues im Raum der Ausstellung oder der Situation des Tragens entstehen, indem sich die Wahrnehmung des Stücks, ob Schmuck oder Artefakt, durch den bewussten Umgang mit den Dingen verändert. In beiden Fällen wird der geschmückte oder betrachtende Mensch auf rationaler und emotionaler Ebene angesprochen und kann dies als Angebot nutzen, sich selbst und sein Sein zu bestätigen oder zu hinterfragen.

own home, and have fun doing so. Yet even if the art of adornment is based on decisions one takes oneself and relates primarily to the self, it still as a rule also would like to communicate or represent something externally. Jewellery can, for instance, refer to both the material and the non-material background of the wearer, his or her education level and tastes shaped by his or her social and ethnic origins. The desire to communicate one's own self-image and to externalise it makes the wearer also continue to be dependent on viewers' perceptions and appraisal. Jewellery only develops its full social impact through reciprocity. Hence the significance of jewellery as a status symbol still exists but the focus is now more strongly on the self, the individual who opts for the jewellery.

The motive of self-representation leads directly to the reason for adorning oneself that is so important nowadays: the search for one's own identity or the desire to design and firmly establish one's identity with the aid of external signs. What is known as contemporary jewellery or auteur jewellery deserves mention in this connection. In this field the creator of the jewellery plays a particular role because s/he incorporates his or her personal history and identity as well as experience and perception of the zeitgeist in designing such works in jewellery. Thus the pieces of jewellery are unequivocally related to the person who created them but are in the best case so polysemic in their symbolic character that they represent for the wearer a supplemental vehicle for self-expression. The viewer, by contrast, is inspired to perceive the piece of jewellery on the one hand in its singularity and, on the other, in relation to the wearer. What in a museum is the space that creates an atmospheric situation for viewing the things in it and inspires reflection is in the case of jewellery the wearer, who gives the piece of jewellery a platform for unfolding its aura by linking various identities – that of the wearer, the viewer and the person who created the jewellery – in the aspect of being adorned.

The experience of visiting a museum and the reasons for wearing jewellery seem, when viewed superficially, to be very far apart indeed. Yet in both cases the focus is on human dealings with objects. The interrelationship between human being and objects causes something new to emerge in the exhibition space or the wearing situation because perception of a piece, be it as jewellery or as an artefact, changes through the conscious handling of things. In both cases the human being, either as wearer or viewer, is addressed on both the rational and the emotional planes and can use this duality as an opportunity to confirm or challenge themself or their own existence.

Erinnerungen
Memories

2016 Brosche | *brooch*
Milchopal, Silber, Edelstahl
milky opal, silver, stainless steel
Anna Storck, BFA Semester 3

Stadtmuseum Simeonstift Trier
City Museum Simeonstift Trier

Das Museum ist ein Ort, um Dinge zu bewahren; ebenso wie die Erinnerungen, die diesen Dingen anhaften. Bewusst oder unbewusst bauen wir Beziehungen zu Objekten auf und verknüpfen sie mit Situationen oder Ereignissen. Sie werden zu Trägern von Erinnerungen und zu Medien zwischenmenschlicher Kommunikation.
Die weißen, leeren Flächen der Bilderrahmen sind ein Angebot, sich an etwas zu erinnern: eine gute Entscheidung, auf der man etwas aufgebaut, oder ein Fehltritt, aus dem man etwas gelernt hat.
Es sind Projektionsflächen, denen jeder von uns einen anderen Inhalt verleiht. Ein Rahmen für die Erinnerungen, die für uns von Bedeutung sind und die wir uns immer wieder ins Gedächtnis rufen wollen.

The museum is a place to preserve things, and also the memories that adhere to these things. Consciously or unconsciously, we build relationships with objects and connect them to situations or events. They become bearers of memories and media for communication between people.
The white, empty surfaces of the picture frames are an invitation to remember something: a good decision on which you have built up something, or a blunder from which you have learned something.
They are projection screens to which each of us imparts different content. A framework for the memories that are important to us, which we would like to recall over and over again.

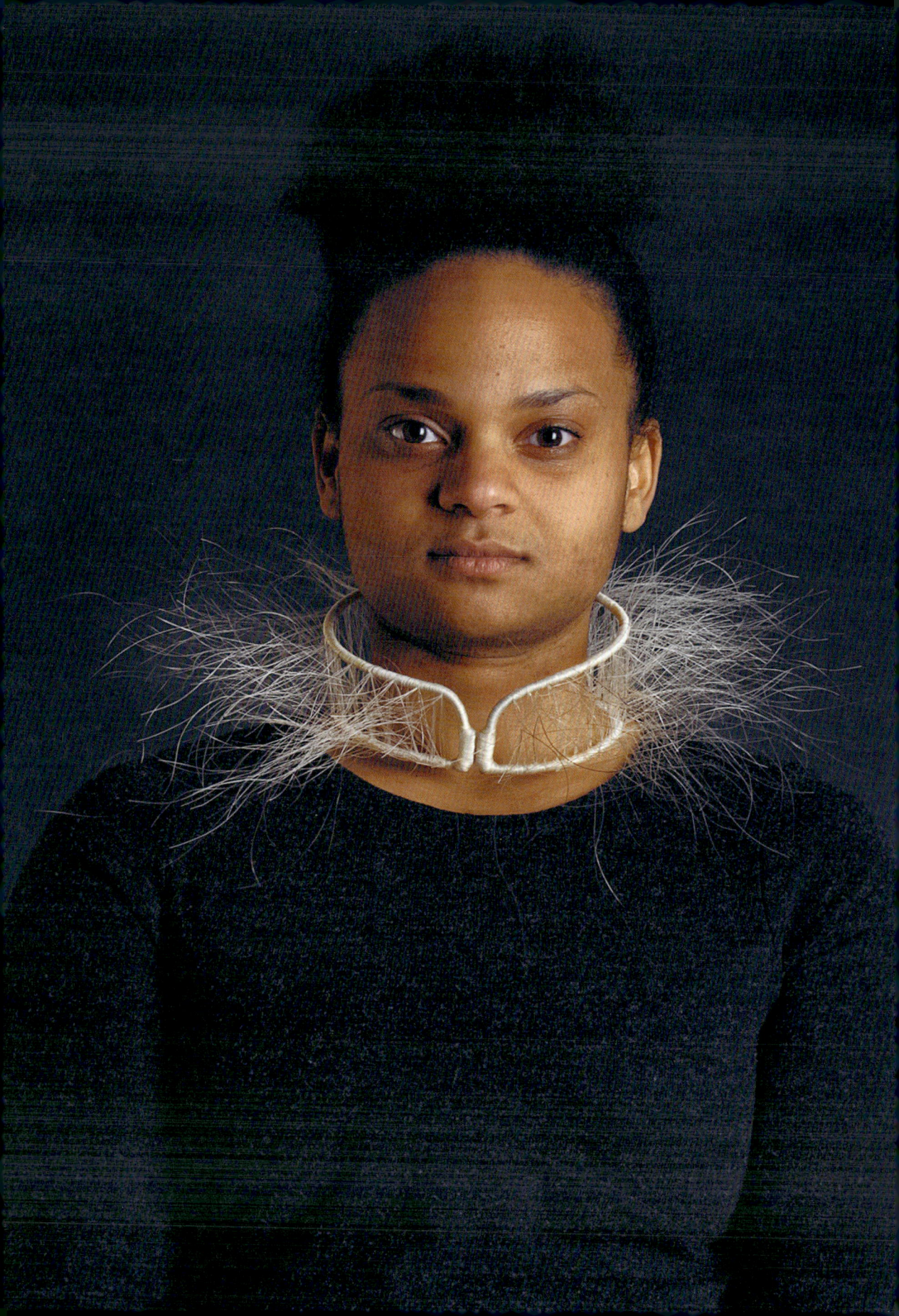

Beffchen | Band

2016 Halsschmuck | *necklace*
Pferdehaar, Stahl | *horsehair, steel*
Tianqi Li, BFA Semester 5

Mich faszinierte eine besondere Form des Kragens – das Beffchen, welches in dem Porträt des Kurfürsten Franz Georg von Schönborn zu sehen ist. Es handelt sich dabei um einen Teil der Amtstracht eines kirchlichen Würdenträgers. Mein Schmuck sollte in ähnlicher Weise durchsichtig sein, aber trotzdem so wirken, als würde er die Kleider, den Körper schützen und so die Würde der Trägerin oder des Trägers bewahren.

Mein Beffchen besteht hauptsächlich aus gewickeltem Pferdehaar. In vielen Kulturen verbindet man mit Materialien aus der Natur die Vorstellung und den Glauben einer schützenden Wirkung. So soll sich die Trägerin oder der Träger meines Kragens von der Natur geschützt fühlen. Die Länge des Pferdehaars stellt den Abstand zur Außenwelt dar. Gleichzeitig wünscht man, es vorsichtig zu berühren, da es zugleich weich, aber auch fest ist. Das Material soll für die Tragenden zugleich schützend und angenehm sein.

I was fascinated by a particular form of collar – the Geneva bands, which can be seen in the portrait of the Prince-Elector Franz Georg von Schönborn. It is part of the official garb of a church dignitary. My jewellery should be similarly transparent but still look as if it would protect the clothes and the body and thus maintain the wearer's dignity.

My Geneva bands are made primarily from coiled horsehair. In many cultures natural materials are linked with the idea of and belief in a protective effect. Thus the wearer of my collar should feel protected by nature. The length of the horsehair represents the distance from the outside world. At the same time you want to touch it carefully because it is simultaneously soft but also firm. The material should be simultaneously protective and comfortable for the wearer.

Porträt des Kurfürsten Franz Georg von Schönborn (reg. 1729–1756), 18. Jh., Ölgemälde | *portrait of Elector Franz Georg von Schönborn (reign: 1729–1756), 18th c., oil painting*
Stadtmuseum Simeonstift Trier, Inv. III 314

Charlestonkleid, Frankreich, um 1924/25, mit Glasperlen bestickter Seidengeorgette, Metallfäden und -spitze | *Charleston dress, France ca. 1924/25, silk georgette embroidered with glass beads, metallic thread and lace*

Stadtmuseum Simeonstift Trier, Inv. VII 853

Glasstein
Glass stone

2016 Halsschmuck | *necklace*
Glas, Silber, Herkimer Diamant
glass, silver, Herkimer diamond
Charlie Cremer, BFA Semester 3

Meine Intention ist es, Edelsteine und Glas zu vereinen. Der Prozess des Verschmelzens von Edelsteinen mit Glas, unter der Einwirkung von hohen Temperaturen, bringt beide Materialien an ihre Grenzen. Häufig kommt es durch das Verschmelzen zu Farbwechseln der Edelsteine und Farbreaktionen mit dem umgebenden Glas.
Für mich spiegelt sich dieses Spannungsverhältnis in dem mit Glasperlen bestickten Abendkleid von 1924/25 wider. Das Zusammenspiel von matt, glänzend und durchscheinend diente mir als Inspirationsquelle. Der Seidengeorgette ist wie das Glas in meinem Anhänger der Träger, der an seine Grenzen gebracht wird. Das Gewicht der aufgenähten Glasperlen ist eine Zerreißprobe für den Stoff. Die Edelsteine stören die Bildung einer stabilen Glasmasse. Deswegen muss ein Gleichgewicht gefunden werden, damit das Perlenkleid sowie die Kette in sich stabil bleiben.

My intention is to unite gemstones and glass. The process of merging gemstones and glass through the effect of high temperatures brings both materials to their limits. Often the fusion results in colour changes in the gemstones and colour reactions with the surrounding glass.
I find this tension reflected in the 1924/25 evening dress decorated with glass beads. The interplay of matt, shiny and translucent inspired me. Like the glass in my pendant, the silk georgette is the carrier taken to its very limits. The weight of the sewn-on glass beads is a tensile test for the fabric. The gemstones disturb the formation of a stable mass of glass. A balance must therefore be found so that both the beaded dress and the necklace remain stable.

Poesie | Poetry

2016 Brosche | *brooch*
Kunststoff, Kupfer, Lack, Edelstahl
plastic, copper, varnish, stainless steel
Denise Ebert, BFA Semester 5

Seit dem Mittelalter ist Trier mit seinen Heiligtümern Ziel für zahlreiche Pilger. Später wurde die Region auch touristisch erschlossen und unter dem Begriff „liebliche Mosel" eine romantisch-verklärte Idealvorstellung geprägt, die im Lauf der Zeit eine gewaltige pittoreske Wirkung entfaltete. In diesem Zusammenhang entstanden kitschig wirkende Souvenirobjekte, wie zum Beispiel Sammelteller aus Keramik, später auch Kunststoff, die „Typisches" der Moselregion wiedergaben. Das Souvenir erinnert an Vergangenes. Es sind kleine, persönliche Erinnerungsstücke für Orte und Personen, denen man sich verbunden fühlt. Durch die Verwendung von Souvenirs in meinen Schmuckstücken möchte ich alten Erinnerungen neuen Glanz verschaffen. Mit diesen geschmückt, trägt man in gewisser Weise seine Erinnerung bei sich.

Trier, with its shrines, has been a destination for many pilgrims since the Middle Ages. Later the region was also opened up touristically and under the expression 'liebliche Mosel' (sweet Moselle) was dominated by a romantic, idealised concept, which as time passed developed a powerful, picturesque impression. Accordingly, souvenir objects emerged, like collectible ceramic and, later also, plastic plates, reproductions of 'typical' items from the Moselle region. Souvenirs recall the past. They are small, personal keepsakes for places and people to which and to whom you feel connected. By using souvenirs in my jewellery I would like to give new lustre to old memories. Wearing this jewellery, in a way you are carrying your memories with you.

Zierteller mit Ansicht der Porta Nigra, Villeroy & Boch Mettlach, um 1840, Feinsteingut mit Kupferstich-Umdruck | *collection plate showing the Porta Nigra, ca. 1840, porcelain with print*
Stadtmuseum Simeonstift Trier, Inv. VIII.377b

Kompression
Compression

2016 Objekt | *object*
medizinische Kompressionsbeklei-dung, Satin, Brokat, Glas-, Kunst-stoff- und Edelsteine, Rettungs-decke, Pflaster, Holz, Plexiglas
medical compression suit, satin, brocade, glass stones, plastic stones, gemstones, rescue blanket, patches, wood, plexiglass
Denise Ebert, BFA Semester 5

Andenkenbild zur Wallfahrt, 1810, Pappe, Seide, Pailletten | *devotional image for pilgrimage, 1810, cardboard, silk, sequin*
Stadtmuseum Simeonstift Trier, Inv. X1085

Das Andenkenbild zur Wallfahrt hat mich auf besondere Weise berührt. Ich verbinde mit einer Wallfahrt eine Reise, bei der das Ziel im Vorder-grund steht. In meinem persönlichen Andenkenbild zeige ich daher meine medizinische Kompressionsbeklei-dung, die die Lösung meiner gesund-heitlichen Probleme zum Ziel hat. Es ist ein Erinnerungsstück, welches einen besonderen Stellenwert in meinem Leben hat.
Ich verbinde mit dieser Kleidung Erleichterung, aber auch eine deut-liche Einschränkung durch den phy-sischen Druck, dem ich ausgesetzt war. Diesen Konflikt habe ich in dem Kastenbild verarbeitet. Im Sinne eines feierlichen Andenkens verkörpert es meine eigene Reise zur Heilung.

In the museum I found the souvenir pictures of pilgrimages uniquely touching. I associate a pilgrimage with a journey where the destination is the focus. That's why in my personal frame I exhibit my medical compression garment, which is the solution in targeting my health problems. It is a memento that has a special significance in my life. I associate this garment with relief, but also with a significant restric-tion through the physical pressure to which I was subjected. I have processed this conflict within my framework. By way of a celebratory keepsake it embodies my own journey to health.

Melancholie
Melancholia

2016 Halsschmuck | *necklace*
Kunststoff, Lava, Hämatit, Silber, Lack, Glitzer | *plastic, lava, hematite, silver, varnish, glitter*
Denise Ebert, BFA Semester 5

Das Stadtmodell im Simeonstift zeigt die Zerstörung der Innenstadt im Jahr 1944. Nach dieser schrecklichen Erfahrung sehnte sich die Bevölkerung nach einer heilen Welt. Diese drückte sich in dem Bedürfnis nach profanen, hübschen sowie kitschigen Dingen aus.
Durch dunkel gehaltene, teils gegensätzliche Materialkombinationen – wie Kohle und Glitzer – möchte ich diese Sehnsucht mit der bitteren Erinnerung in einen Zusammenhang bringen und ihr Ausdruck verleihen. Schmuck kann zwischen Menschen und Umwelt vermitteln, ermöglicht über die Erinnerung und den Souvenircharakter eine Kommunikation und Interaktion zwischen Kulturen, Völkern sowie Einzelpersonen. Indem man über das Schmuckstück spricht, entsteht eine gemeinschaftsstiftende Erinnerung, welche die Brüche der Vergangenheit zu überwinden hilft.

The city model in the Simeonstift Museum shows the destruction of the city centre in 1944. After this terrible experience, the population longed for an ideal world and this was expressed in the need for mundane, pretty and kitsch things.
Through dark, partly contradictory combinations of materials, such as coal and glitter, I would like to bring this longing and the bitter memories into one context and give it expression. Jewellery can mediate between people and the environment; through memory and its souvenir-like character it facilitates a communication and interaction between cultures and peoples as well as individuals. Talking about the piece of jewellery creates a communal memory that helps to heal the fractures of the past.

Joachim Woditsch, Modell von der zerstörten Stadt Trier, 2001, Holz
Joachim Woditsch, model of destroyed City of Trier, 2001, wood

Maske | Mask

2016 Körperschmuck | *body related object*
Spiegel, Messing | *mirror, brass*
Vanessa Zöller, BFA Semester 3

Schandmaske, 17. Jh., Eisen
scold's bridle, 17th c., iron
Stadtmuseum Simeonstift Trier, Inv. X 791b

Die Schandmaske ist ein mittelalterliches Folterinstrument.
Die Schandmaske verstärkt den Verlust der Ehre des Beschuldigten.
Die Schandmaske veranschaulicht die begangene Tat.

Ich habe meine Maske passgenau auf meinen Körper angefertigt.
Ich allein zwinge mich, sie zu tragen.
Ich konfrontiere mich mit mir selbst, das ist unbequem.
Ich blicke prüfend in mich.

Ich bekenne die Schande, dass ich mich nicht gut verhalten habe.
Ich habe mich entehrt.
Durch meine Ausflüchte, durch meine Unaufrichtigkeit, durch meine Unzulänglichkeit.

Darum will ich mich reinigen.
Geheilt aus dieser Prüfung hervorgehen.

The Schandmaske is a medieval torture instrument.
The Schandmaske intensifies the accused's loss of honour.
The Schandmaske illustrates the crime committed.

I have made my mask to fit my body.
I alone compel myself to wear it.
I confront myself, which is uncomfortable.
I look searchingly into myself.

I confess the shame for not behaving well.
I have dishonoured myself.
Through my excuses, through my insincerity, through my inadequacy.

Therefore I want to cleanse myself.
Emerge healed from this test.

Schutz | Protection

2016 Halsschmuck | *necklace*
Stein, Leder | *stone, leather*
Tianqi Li, BFA Semester 5

Meister Steffann, Steipenriese, 1483, Sandstein | *Master Steffann, Steipe knight, 1483, sandstone*
Stadtmuseum Simeonstift Trier, Inv. I 0024

Meine Inspiration war die Skulpturengruppe der geharnischten Ritter im Eingangsbereich des Stadtmuseums, die ursprünglich an der dem Dom zugewandten Fassade der sogenannten Steipe angebracht war. An zentraler Stelle der Stadt, dem Marktplatz, drückten sie den Willen zur Verteidigung bürgerlicher Rechte und Freiheiten aus. Die Statuen und damit auch der Harnisch sind aus Sandstein gearbeitet. Dies inspirierte mich dazu, mein Stück aus Marmor zu schleifen.

Marmor ist weiß, undurchsichtig und weich. Er wirkt auf mich ruhig, rein, heilig, aber auch wie eine gemütliche Bekleidung, die man anziehen möchte. Die Außenform des Steins habe ich beibehalten, nur die Innenseite ist von mir bearbeitet worden. Am Anfang wollte ich das Äußere in Form einer Hand schleifen. Doch erschien mir die Innenseite wichtiger als die äußere Form. Nur die Trägerin oder der Träger soll um die Bedeutung der eingravierten Hände wissen: So ist die Kette ein zuverlässiger Freund, der mich in den Armen hält, um mich zu schützen.

I was inspired by the sculptural group of the knights in armour in the entrance of the City Museum, which was originally attached to the cathedral-facing façade of the so-called Steipe. In the market square, in the heart of the city, it expressed the will to defend civil rights and freedoms. The statues and therefore also the armour are made from sandstone, which inspired me to carve my piece from marble.

Marble is white, opaque and soft. I find it peaceful, clean, holy, but also like a piece of comfortable clothing that you would like to wear. I retained the exterior shape of the stone and only worked on the inside. To start with I wanted to grind the outside into the shape of a hand. But the inside seemed more important than the external shape. Only the wearer is to know the importance of the engraved hands: the chain is a dependable friend, holding me in its arms, to protect me.

Münder | Mouths

2016 Objekte | *objects*
Gips, Metall | *plaster, metal*
Gina-Nadine Müller, BFA Semester 1

Hello? Talking..
People
How are you?
Who are you?
What's the matter?
Post-
Latest news
Gossip
Publicity
Share.
What does really matter?
Content,
Impact.

Ferdinand Tietz, Saturn-Statue aus dem Skulpturenzyklus des Kurfürstlichen Palais Trier, um 1758/60, Sandstein | *Ferdinand Tietz, saturn statue from the sculpture cycle of the Kurfürstliche Palais Trier, ca. 1758/60, sandstone*
Stadtmuseum Simeonstift Trier, Inv. I.4

Der Mund hat eine starke Wirkung. Er steht für Kommunikation. Im Stadtmuseum Simeonstift begegnet man einer Vielzahl an Mündern. Einer der auffallendsten ist der Mund der Saturnfigur von Ferdinand Tietz: Fehlende und schiefe Zähne sind von Tietz nicht beschönigt, sondern betont worden. Sie zeigen das Alter der dargestellten Person und ihre Menschlichkeit.
Dieser Mund ist die Grundlage meiner Wandinstallation. Die Kopien ähneln einander, sind jedoch nicht identisch. Zusammen bilden sie eine Einheit, einen Chor.
Zentraler Lebensinhalt aller Lebewesen ist der Austausch mit anderen. Menschen sind weltweit vernetzt, die Vielstimmigkeit ist groß. Kann Kommunikation zu viel werden? Reden wir miteinander oder aneinander vorbei? Worüber reden wir?

The mouth has a powerful effect. It stands for communication. In the City Museum Simeonstift one encounters a multitude of mouths. One of the most striking is the mouth of Ferdinand Tietz's Saturn figure: Tietz has not glossed over missing and crooked teeth but rather emphasised them. They show the age of the person represented and their humanity. This mouth is the basis of my wall installation. The copies resemble each other but are not identical. Together they form a unit, a choir. Exchange with others is central to the lives of all living things. People are networked across the world; there is a great multitude of voices. Can communication become too much? Do we talk to each other or past each other? What do we talk about?

Karl Marx

2015 Porträt | *portrait*
Styropor, Ton | *styrofoam, clay*
John Maddox, BFA Semester 1

Willi Sitte, Karl Marx, undatiert, Öl auf Hartfaser | *Willi Sitte, Karl Marx, undated, oil on hardboard*
Dauerleihgabe der | *permanent loan from* Bundesrepublik Deutschland

Während meiner Schulzeit sowohl in ConUS (Continental United States) als auch im Ausland (Deutschland, Chile) wurde die Erwähnung kommunistischer Ideen oder Menschen, die mit dem Kommunismus im Zusammenhang gesehen wurden, als unamerikanisch abgestempelt und mit dem Bösen gleichgesetzt, wenn es überhaupt thematisiert wurde. Aus den gelegentlichen, schwachen Versuchen meiner Mitschüler, den Vorhang zu heben, wurde mir klar, dass ich keine unvoreingenommenen Informationen bekommen würde. Individuelles Streben nach Informationen über diese „Sache" wurde abgewehrt, und wer unvorsichtig war, konnte als „commy", Staatsfeind, bezeichnet werden. Erst nachdem ich das „Land of the Free" verlassen habe, begegnete ich einer Meinungsvielfalt in dieser früher unansprechbaren Angelegenheit.

In ConUS: Was?
In the ConUS: Marx – Marxismus, Kommunisten… Terroristen!
In ConUS: Laut – totgeschwiegen… Der Freiheit wegen.
In ConUS: Frage – aus Kindesmund: Marx, wer ist… ssshhh, ruhig!
In ConUS: Marx – Schlag Wort… Herr Lehrer??? Kopf gesenkt.
In ConUS: Kauernd – lauernd.
In the Continental United States – Land of the Free.

In all my years in school, both in ConUS (Continental United States) and abroad (Germany, Chile), the mention of communism or individuals associated with communism was heavily labelled as un-American and therefore evil, if it was mentioned at all! From the occasionally feeble attempts of some of my fellow students I soon came to realise that no unbiased information would be forthcoming. Individual pursuit of information was discouraged, and if you weren't careful you could be labelled a Commie, an enemy of the state. Only after leaving the 'land of the free' did I encounter a variety of opinions on this matter.

In ConUS: What?
In the ConUS: Marx – Marxism, Communists… terrorists!
In ConUS: Loud – hushed up… for the sake of freedom.
In ConUS: Question – from a child's mouth: Who is Marx? Shh, quiet!
In ConUS: Marx – catchword… Mr Teacher??? Head down.
In ConUS: Cowering – lurking.
In the Continental United States – land of the free.

Rahmen | Frames

2016 Installation | *installation*
Kunststoff, Fotografie | *plastic, photography*
Maximilian Schröder, BFA Semester 3

Rahmen des Porträts des Kurfürsten Franz Georg von Schönborn (reg. 1729–1756) | *frame of Portrait of Elector Franz Georg von Schönborn (reign: 1729–1756)*

Gemälderahmen haben meist einen ornamentalen Charakter. Aus Holz geschnitzt oder Marmor gemeißelt wurden sie anschließend vergoldet. Ich möchte diesen aufwendig gestalteten Rahmen mehr Beachtung schenken, denn meist steht das Bild oder Portrait im Mittelpunkt und nimmt den Rahmen die Aufmerksamkeit. Für mich stellt die Anordnung der Elemente des Rahmens erst eine Situation her, welche der Betrachterin oder dem Betrachter die Schönheit des Bildes bewusst macht und die Bedeutung der dargestellten Person oder des Gegenstandes erzeugt. Dies kann man analog zu dem kosmischen System sehen, in dem die Sonne im Zentrum liegt. Die Vielfalt der Rahmen und ihre Schönheit haben mich fasziniert. Ich wollte ein Objekt schaffen, welches die Rahmen in den Fokus der Betrachterin oder des Betrachters rückt. Meine Installation überführt die Rahmen von den Wänden in den Raum. Der Mensch kann in sie eintreten und sich selbst in das Zentrum des Kosmos stellen.

Picture frames are usually ornamental in character, carved from wood or sculpted from marble then subsequently gilded. I want to give this elaborately designed frame more consideration, as the picture or portrait is usually the focal point and takes attention away from the frame. To my mind, the arrangement of the elements of a frame produces a situation which makes the viewer aware of the beauty of the picture and defines the person or object represented. This can be seen in analogy to the cosmic system in which the sun lies at the centre.
The diversity of the frames and their beauty fascinated me. I wanted to create an object which made the frames the focal point of the observer. My installation transferred the frames from the walls into the room. A person can step into it and place themselves at the centre of the cosmos.

Sammlung
Collection

2016 Collier | *necklace*
Kunststoff, Fotografie, Messing
plastic, photography, brass
Maximilian Schröder, BFA Semester 3

Daktyliothek, 17. Jh., Holz, Gemmen, Steine, Elfenbein
Dactyliotheca, 17th c., wood, carved gems, stones, ivory
Stadtmuseum Simeonstift Trier, Inv. X 958

Im Altertum und in der Renaissance wurden in einer Daktyliothek neben außergewöhnlich geschliffenen Steinen auch Gemmen und Kameen gesammelt. Letztere wurden ursprünglich als Siegelsteine zur Beglaubigung von Urkunden und wichtigen Schriftstücken verwendet. Sie dienten der Identifikation.

Auch Schmuck kann zur Identifikation dienen. Er gibt Auskunft über die soziale Distinktion der Trägerin oder des Trägers, seinen Stand sowie seine gesellschaftliche Zugehörigkeit. Die Einzigartigkeit der Schmuckobjekte aus den unterschiedlichsten Bereichen im Museum hat mich dazu inspiriert, diese zu fotografieren, ihre Abbilder zu sammeln und zu einer tragbaren Daktyliothek zusammenzuführen. Es ist ein opulentes Spiel mit Identitäten, welches zugleich den klassischen Juwelenschmuck neu interpretiert.

In antiquity and during the Renaissance exceptionally cut stones were collected in a dactyliotheca alongside intaglios and cameos. The latter were originally used as seal stones for the authentication of certificates and important documents. They served as identification.

Jewellery can also serve as identification. It provides information about the social distinction of the wearer and their status as well as their social affiliation. The uniqueness of the pieces of jewellery from the various parts of the museum inspired me to photograph them and to collect the photos together in a portable dactyliotheca. It is an opulent game of identity whilst at the same time provides a new interpretation of classical jewellery.

Kragen | Collar

2016 Halsschmuck | necklace
Tampons, Garn | *tampons, thread*
Stefanie Thalhammer,
BFA Semester 3

Daniel Block, Bildnis einer Bürgerin, 1636, Öl auf Leinwand
Daniel Block, Portrait of a Citizen, 1636, oil on canvas
Stadtmuseum Simeonstift Trier, Inv. III.228

In unserer Gesellschaft wird das Thema Menstruation tabuisiert. Wenn in der Werbung darüber gesprochen wird, taucht die Menstruation als etwas Unreines auf, etwas, was man unsichtbar machen sollte. Damit wird der Gesellschaft suggeriert, dass die Periode mit Scham behaftet ist. Viele Frauen nehmen die Menstruation einfach hin, ohne wirklich zu wissen, was in ihrem Körper passiert.

Der Mühlsteinkragen ist eine Modeerscheinung des 16. Jahrhunderts. Vorwiegend wurde er von Frauen und Männern der gehobenen Gesellschaftsschicht als Bestandteil der Ausgehkleidung getragen. Mit dem Kragen aus Tampons, den die Träger und Trägerinnen mit Stolz tragen sollen, habe ich versucht, dem Thema Menstruation mehr Ansehen und Würde zu verleihen: denn die Menstruation ist eine wichtige, einzigartige und faszinierende Phase, die der weibliche Körper durchläuft. Es ist ein notwendiger Prozess für die menschliche Existenz.

In our society menstruation is a taboo topic. When reference is made in advertising, menstruation appears as something unclean, something which should be made invisible. Thus society is persuaded that periods are something shameful. Many women simply accept menstruation without really knowing what is happening in their bodies.

The ruff is a fashionable trend from the sixteenth century. It was predominantly worn by upper-class men and women as part of their evening wear. With the collar of tampons, which the wearer should wear proudly, I have tried to confer more esteem and dignity on the theme of menstruation, because menstruation is an important, unique and fascinating phase which the female body goes through. It is a necessary process for human existence.

Gebet | Prayer

2016 Halskette | *necklace*
Gips, Stahl | *plaster, steel*
Rinke Wassenberg, BFA Semester 3

Trotz der großen Unterschiede zwischen der christlichen und islamischen Religion gibt es auch viele Gemeinsamkeiten. Diese habe ich untersucht und daraus sind diese Schmuckstücke entstanden. Besonders inspiriert haben mich die Gebetsketten in beiden Religionen. Die Schmuckstücke sind in der Formgebung so gehalten, dass sie gut in der Hand liegen und man sie zur Meditation nutzen könnte. Ich habe zwei Hälften der gleichen Form aneinander gefügt, die jedoch aus verschiedenen Materialien bestehen, wobei je eine Hälfte für eine Religion steht. Während meiner Arbeit habe ich versucht, mir einen neutralen Blick auf die Religionen zu bewahren. Denn wir Menschen sind alle gleich.

Despite the big differences between the Christian and Islamic religions, there are also many similarities, my study of which resulted in these pieces of jewellery. I was particularly inspired by the prayer beads found in both religions.
The pieces are so designed that they lie nicely in the hand and can be used for meditation. I have joined two halves of the same shape together, each from a different material with each half representing a religion. Whilst I was working, I tried to keep a neutral view of the religions. Because all people are the same.

Kalligraphie einer Koransure, 2007, Druck auf Metall | *calligraphy of a sura from the Koran, 2007, print on metal*

Leihgabe des | *loan from* Islamischen Kulturzentrum Trier e.V.

Turmmonstranz, 15. Jh., Kupfer, versilbert und vergoldet, Glas
tower monstrance, 15th c., silver- and gold-plated copper, glass
Stadtmuseum Simeonstift Trier, Inv. X 974

Monstranz
Monstrance

2016 Halsschmuck | *necklace*
Kunststoff, Kalkstein, Bergkristall, Flachsgarn | *plastic, limestone, rock crystal, flax twine*
Valérie Wagner, BFA Semester 5

Ich bin von der gotischen Monstranz ausgegangen, in der die Reliquie im Zentrum steht, denn sie macht das Heilige anschaulich. Die Schmuckfassung dieser Objekte vermittelt durch das Strahlen der Steine und des Goldes den Moment des Heiligen. Als ich die Monstranz sah, stellte ich mir folgende Fragen:
Was ist für mich heutzutage heilig? Was braucht Schutz und Verehrung? Mein Schmuckstück, welches aus Kalkstein besteht, der um Bergkristalle gewachsen ist, stellt für mich ein Symbol einer sehr besonderen Uhr dar: die des Rhythmus des Lebens, der Natur, des Wachstums. Die Kette ist zugleich Reliquie und Reliquiar der Zeit, die uns heute zu schnell davon rennt. Der Träger selbst wird zum heiligen Reliquiar, denn er umschließt seinen eigenen natürlichen Zeitrhythmus, der durch das kontemplative Betrachten des Schmucks erweckt wird.

My starting point was the gothic monstrance – which has the relic at its centre – because the holy object is clearly visible. Through the radiance of its stones and gold, the object's setting conveys the holiness of the moment. When I saw the monstrance I asked myself the following questions: What is holy for me today? What requires protection and worship? My piece of jewellery, made from limestone which grew around rock crystals, represents a very special clock to me, a clock for the rhythm of life, of nature, of growth. The chain is simultaneously a relic and a reliquary of time, which runs away from us too fast these days. The wearer themself becomes a holy reliquary, encompassing their own natural rhythm of time, which is awakened by looking at the jewellery in contemplation.

Stein
Stone
Schmuck
Jewellery
Kunst
Art
2006–2016

2012 Halsschmuck | *necklace*
Aquamarin, Smaragd, Kunststoff, Lack, Silber, Stahl | *aquamarine, emerald, plastic, varnish, silver, steel*
Matthias Dyer, Diplom Graduation work

2012 Halsschmuck | *necklace*
Lapislazuli, Kunststoff, Lack, Silber, Stahl | *lapis lazuli, plastic, varnish, silver, steel*
Matthias Dyer, Diplom Graduation work

2016 Objekte | *objects*
Basalt | *basalt*
Vesal Bahmani Nik, MFA Semester 2

2015 Halsschmuck | *necklace*
Achat, Labradorit, Silber | *agate, labradorite, silver*
Franziska Seilern-Aspang, BFA Graduation work

2015 Halsschmuck | *necklace*
Silber, Bergkristall, Wolle | *silver, rock crystal, wool*
Franziska Seilern-Aspang, BFA Graduation work

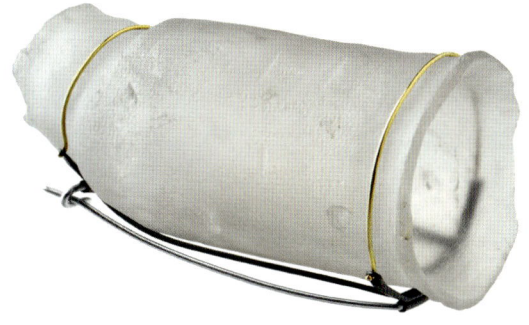

2014 „Guts 1" Brosche | *brooch*
Gold, Silber, Stahl, Quarz | *gold, silver, steel, quartz*
Nicolas Estrada, MFA Graduation work

2014 „Das kleine Boot hat schon tausende Berge hinter sich gelassen" Brosche | *brooch*
Silber, Farbe, Fundstück, Edelstahl | *silver, paint, found object, stainless steel*
Tala Yuan, MFA Graduation work

2014 „DuMu-Brücke" Halsschmuck | *necklace*
Blattgold, Messing, Farbe | *gold leaf, brass, paint*
Tala Yuan, MFA Graduation work

2012 „Efeu" Halsschmuck | *necklace*
Efeublätter, Stahl, Harz | *ivy leaves, steel, resin*
Carmen Hauser, MA Graduation work

2012 „Schattenwelt II" Brosche | *brooch*
Erde, Harz, geschwärztes Silber | *soil, resin, blackened silver*
Carmen Hauser, MA Graduation work

2012 Broschen | *brooches*
Ginkgo-, Kirsch-, Ahorn- und Buchenblätter, Harz, Gold | *ginkgo, cherry, maple and beech leaves, resin, gold*
Carmen Hauser, MA Graduation work

2014 Fotografie | photography
Anastasiya Larionova, BFA Semester 3

2015 „Adrenalin kickt IO" Fotomontage | *photomontage*
Vanessa Zöller, BFA Semester 1

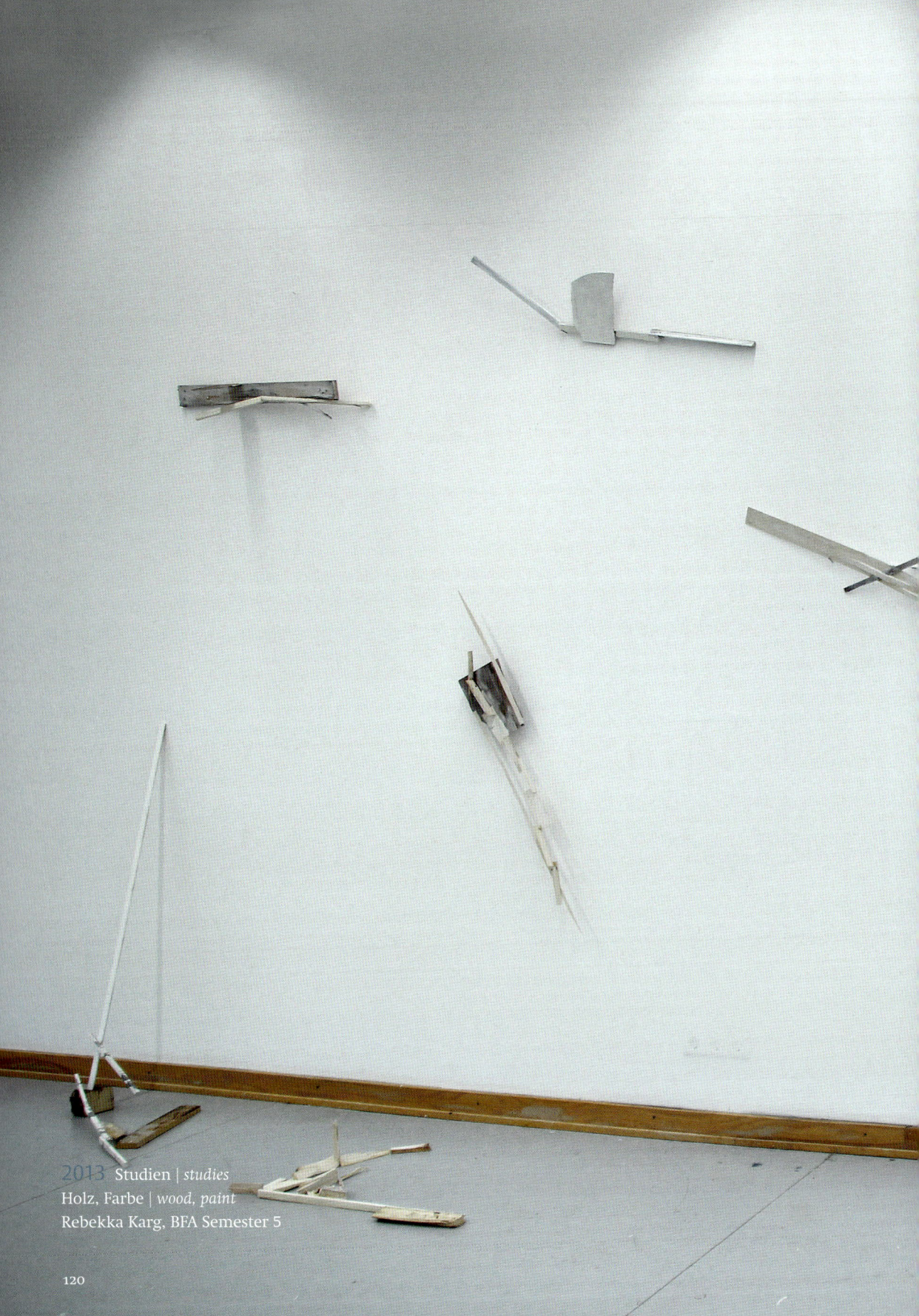

2013 Studien | *studies*
Holz, Farbe | *wood, paint*
Rebekka Karg, BFA Semester 5

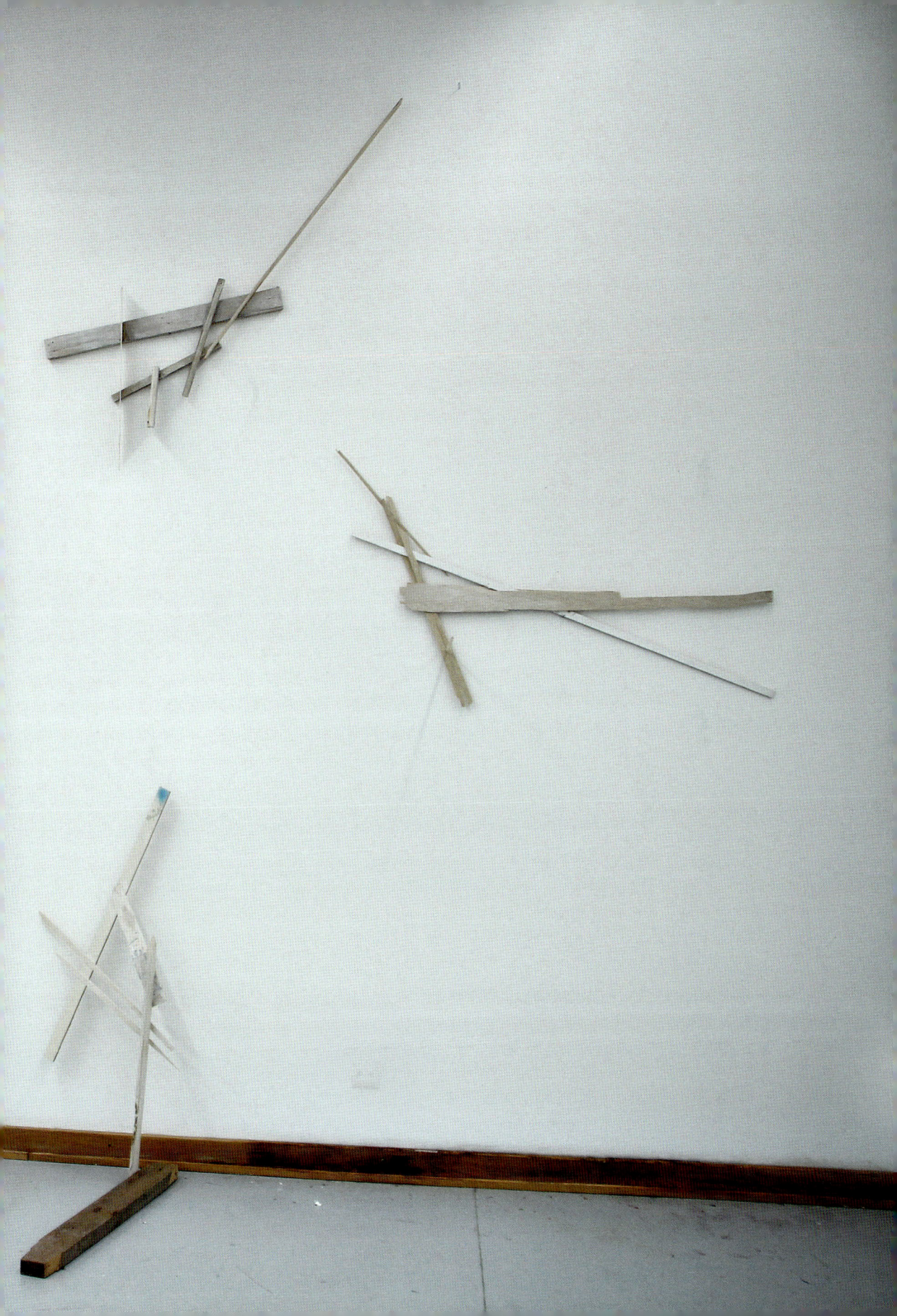

2014 Halsschmuck | *necklace*
Kupfer, Emaille, Silber | *copper, enamel, silver*
Rebekka Karg, BFA Graduation work

2014 Halsschmuck | *necklace*
Kupfer, Emaille, Silber | *copper, enamel, silver*
Rebekka Karg, BFA Graduation work

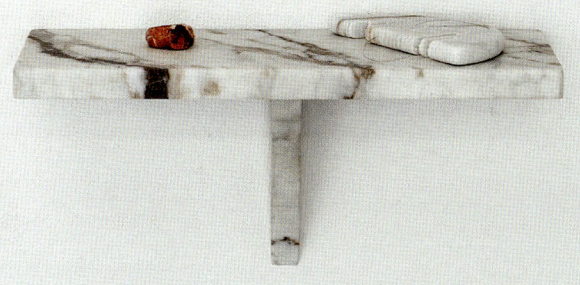

2014 Installation | *installation*
Marmor | *marble*
Pornruedee Boonyapan, MFA Graduation work

Installation | *installation*
Acrylglas, Eisen, Meersalz | *acrylic glass, iron, sea salt*
Pornruedee Boonyapan, MFA Graduation work

2014 „Rückenstück" Objekt | *object*
Basalt | *basalt*
Nina Fuchsberger, BFA Graduation work

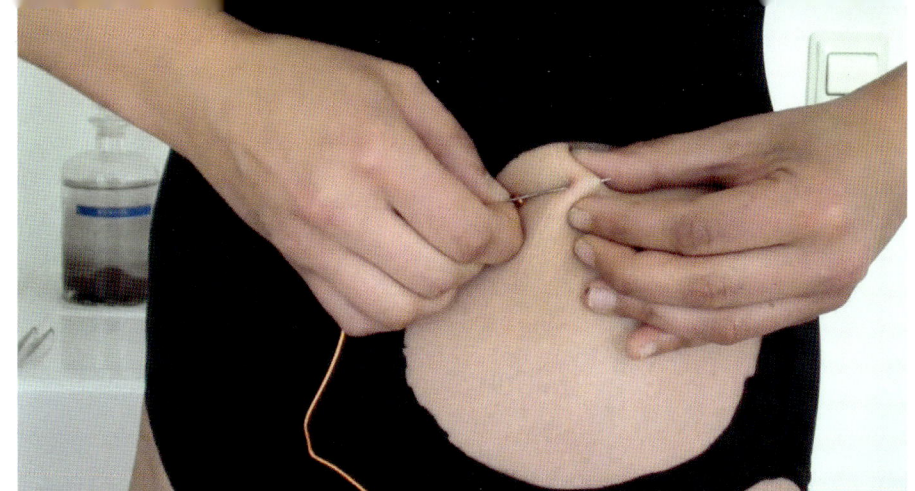
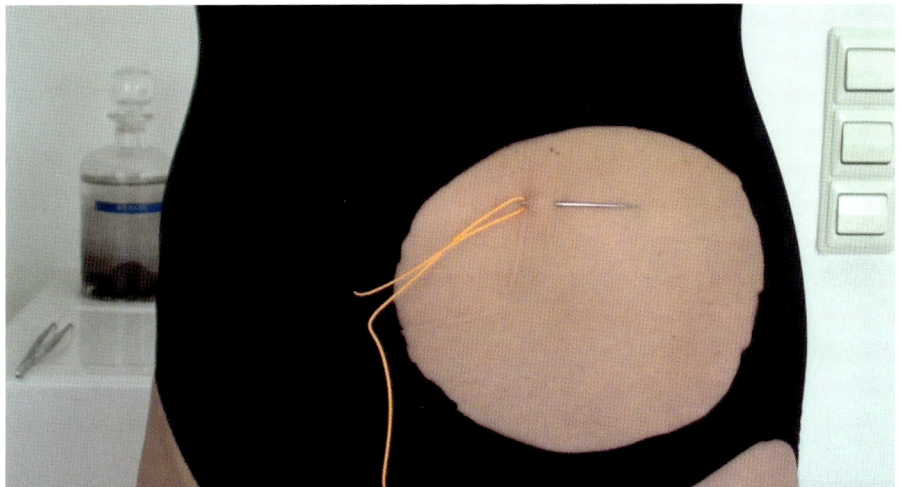
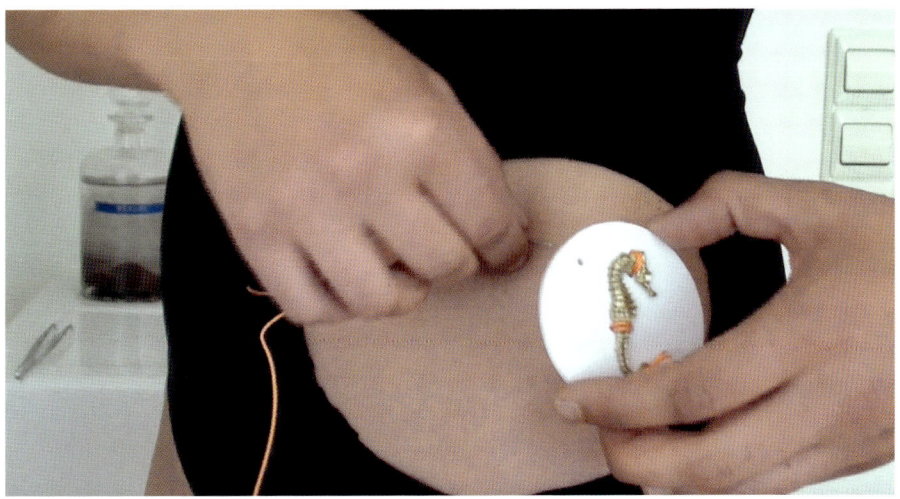

2014 „Seepferdchen" Video | *video*
Video still | *video still*
Nina Fuchsberger, BFA Graduation work

2012 „Feuer und Stein" Brosche | *brooch*
Arkansas, Silber, Edelstahl | *arkansas, silver, stainless steel*
Hye-Shil Kim, Diplom Graduation work

2012 Halsschmuck | *necklace*
Obsidian, Silber | *obsidian, silver*
Hye-Shil Kim, Diplom Graduation work

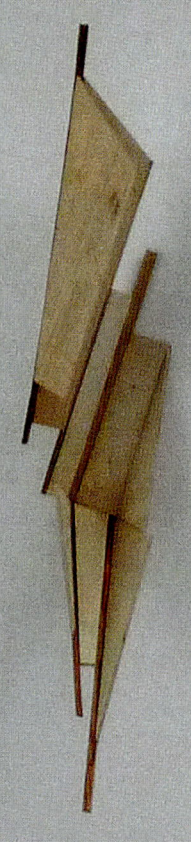

2013 Objekte | *objects*
Holz, Gips, Farbe | *wood, plaster, paint*
Edu Tarín, MFA Semester 2

2016 Halsschmuck | *necklace*
Gießharz, Silber, Gold, Tinte, PVC | *resin, silver, gold, ink, PVC*
Mahvash Salim Raza, MFA Graduation work

2015 Halsschmuck | *necklace*
Gießharz, Silber, Tinte, PVC | *resin, silver, ink, PVC*
Mahvash Salim Raza, MFA Graduation work

2009 „Sperrmüll" Fotomontage | *photomontage*
Matthias Dyer, Diplom Semester 2

2011 „Crème-Rood" Halsschmuck | *necklace*
Filz, Messing | *felt, brass*
Anneke Bloemers, Diplom Graduation work

2014 „1802440080"
Halsschmuck | *necklace*
Stephie-Stein, Kunststoff | *Stephie-Stein, plastic*
Stephanie Morawetz, BFA Graduation work

2014 „60233040"
Halsschmuck | *necklace*
Stephie-Stein, Magnete | *Stephie-Stein, magnets*
Stephanie Morawetz, BFA Graduation work

2014 Objekte | *objects*
Diverse Materialien | *mixed materials*
Tala Yuan, MFA Semester 3

2007 Anhänger | *pendants*
Perlen, Gold | *pearls, gold*
Sabine Wehr, Diplom Semester 7

2007 Gravur | *engraving*
Fluorit | *fluorite*
Sabine Wehr, Diplom Graduation work

2007 "Sommerperlen" Halsschmuck | *necklace*
Gräser, Quiltgarn | *grass, thread*
Sina Emrich, Diplom Graduation work

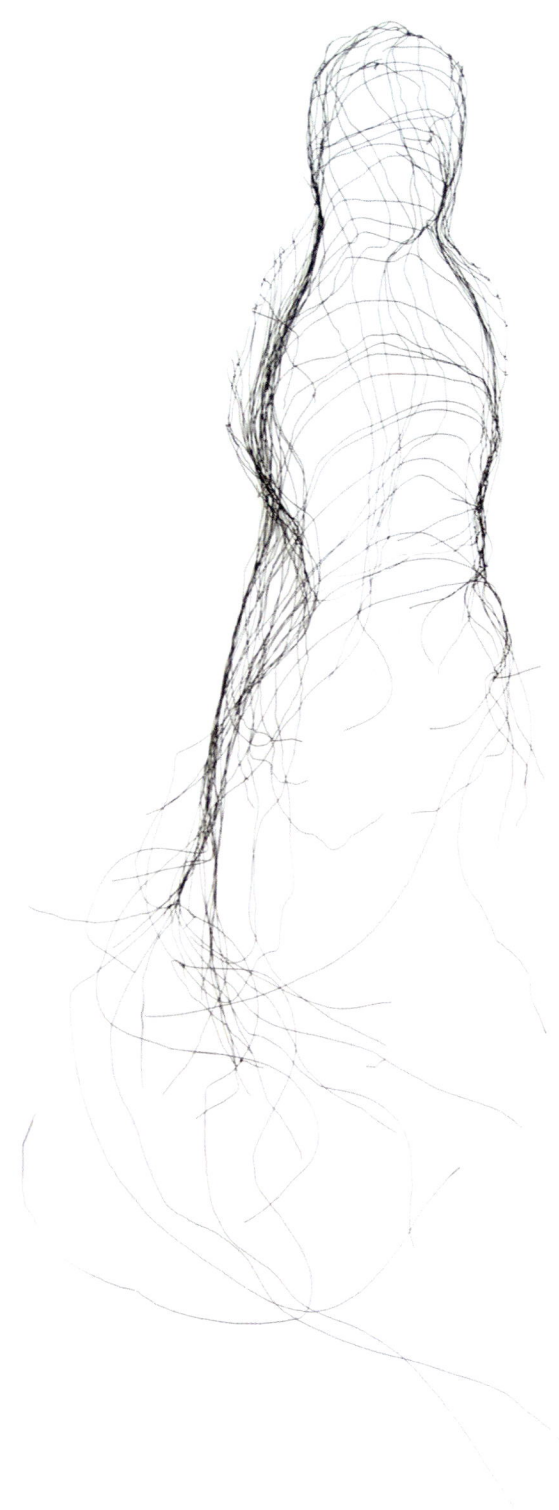

2016 „alter ego" Objekt | *object*
Stahl | *steel*
Sonia Pibernat, MFA Semester 1

2015 „Mold C1" Halsschmuck | *necklace*
Granit, Silber, Textil | *granite, silver, textile*
Edu Tarín, MFA Graduation work

2012 „revival 5" Brosche | *brooch*
vergoldetes Kupfer | *gold plated copper*
Edu Tarín, BA Graduation work

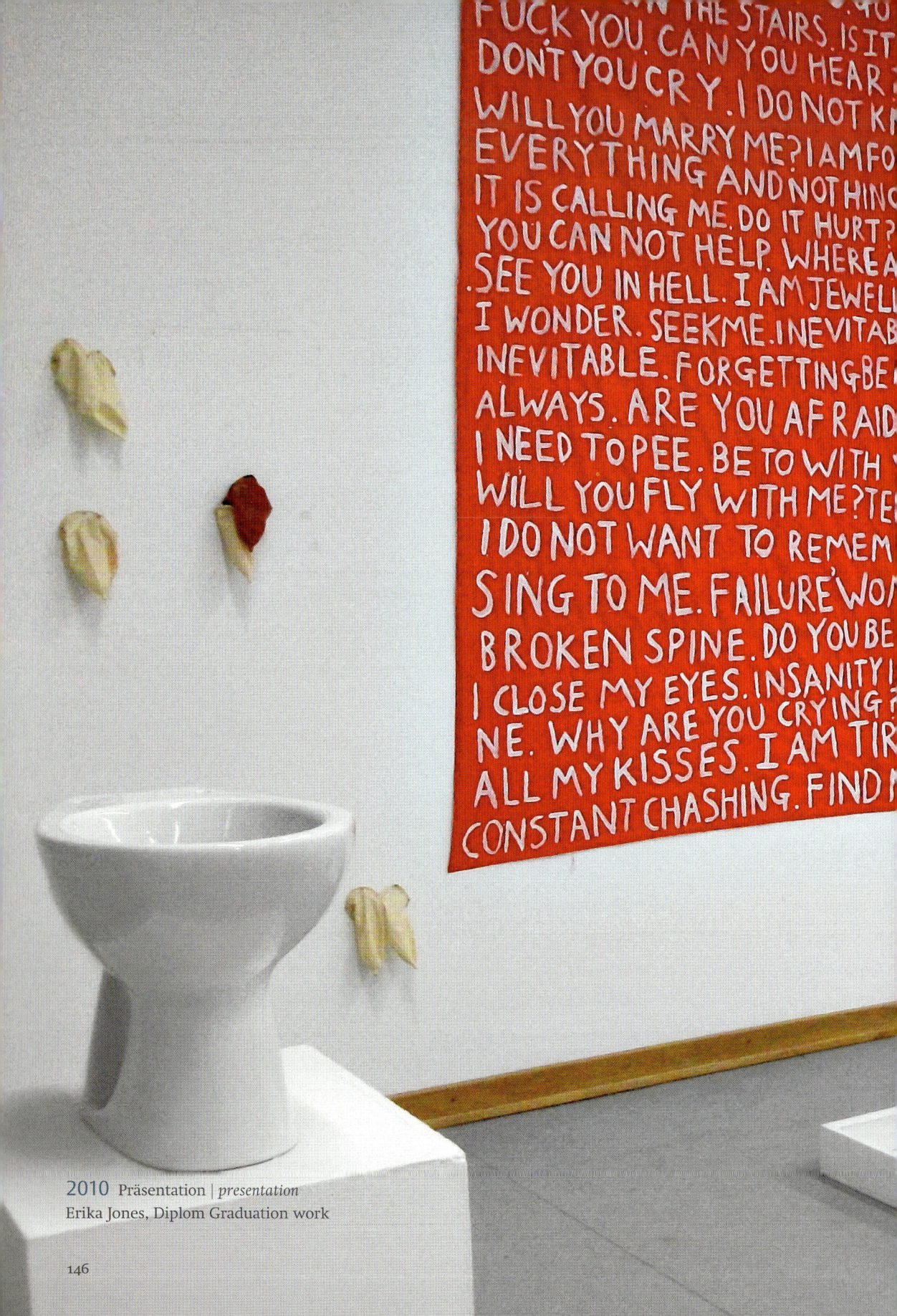

2010 Präsentation | *presentation*
Erika Jones, Diplom Graduation work

2010 „Do you See too?" Objekt | *object*
Metall, Garn, Farbe | *metal, thread, paint*
Erika Jones, Diplom Graduation work

2010 „A Beautiful Piece of Jewellery" Installation | *installation*
Toilette, Farbe | *toilet, paint*
Erika Jones, Diplom Graduation work

2010 „Remains of a Promise Never to Be Broken?" Objekte | *objects*
Steine, Holz, Kupfer, Emaille, Farbe | *stones, wood, copper, enamel, paint*
Erika Jones, Diplom Graduation work

2010 Zeichnung | *drawing*
Farbe auf Bettlaken | paint *on bedsheet*
Erika Jones, Diplom Graduation work

2013 „Schmuck nervt" Fotografie | *photography*
Nina Fuchsberger, BFA Semester 3

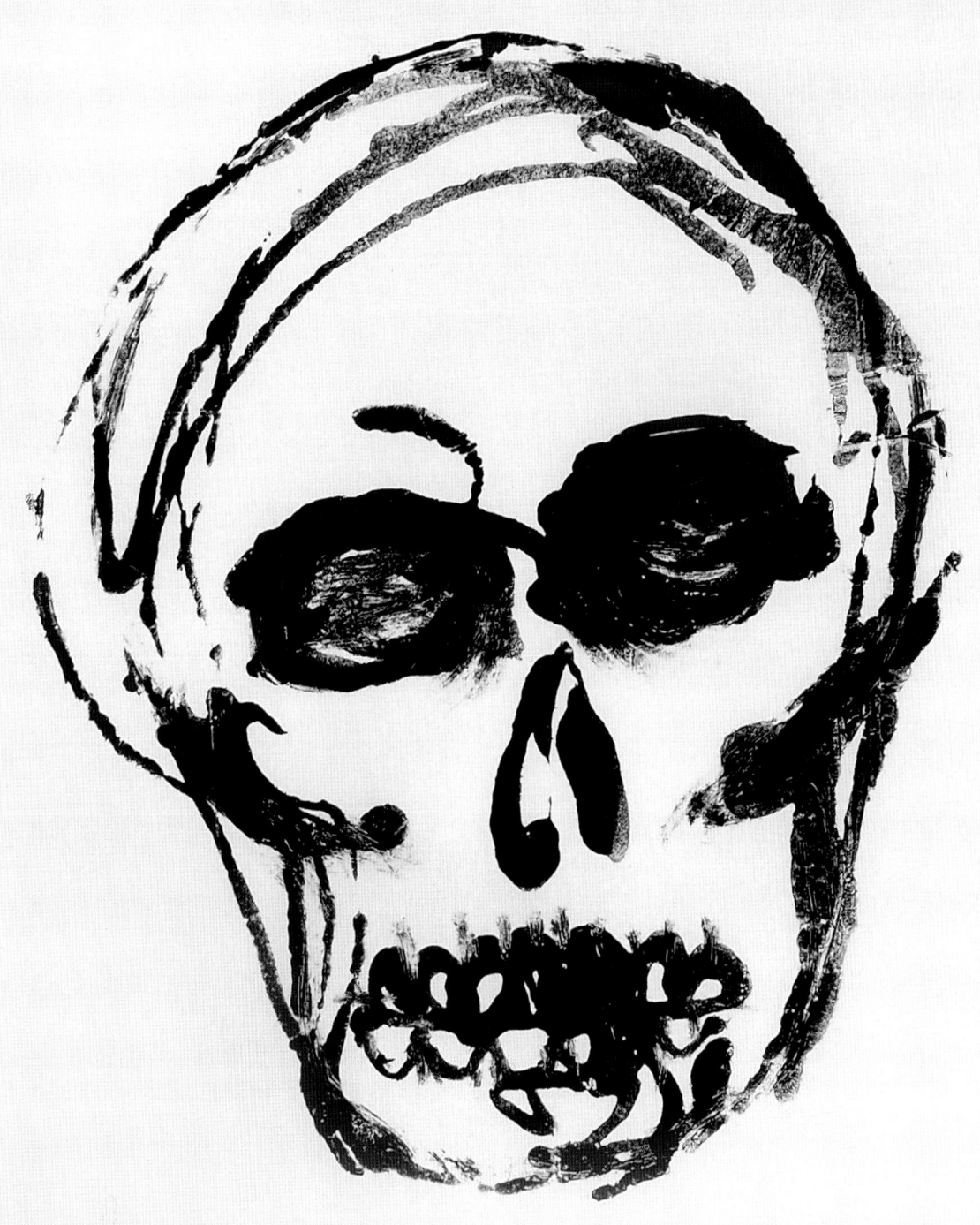

2015 Zeichnung | *drawing*
Tusche auf Papier | *indian ink on paper*
Carolin Denter, BFA Semester 3

2010 „Hanging by a Thread II + IV" Broschen | *brooches*
Recon®, Seide, Stahl | *Recon®, silk, steel*
Javier Moreno Frías, MA Graduation work

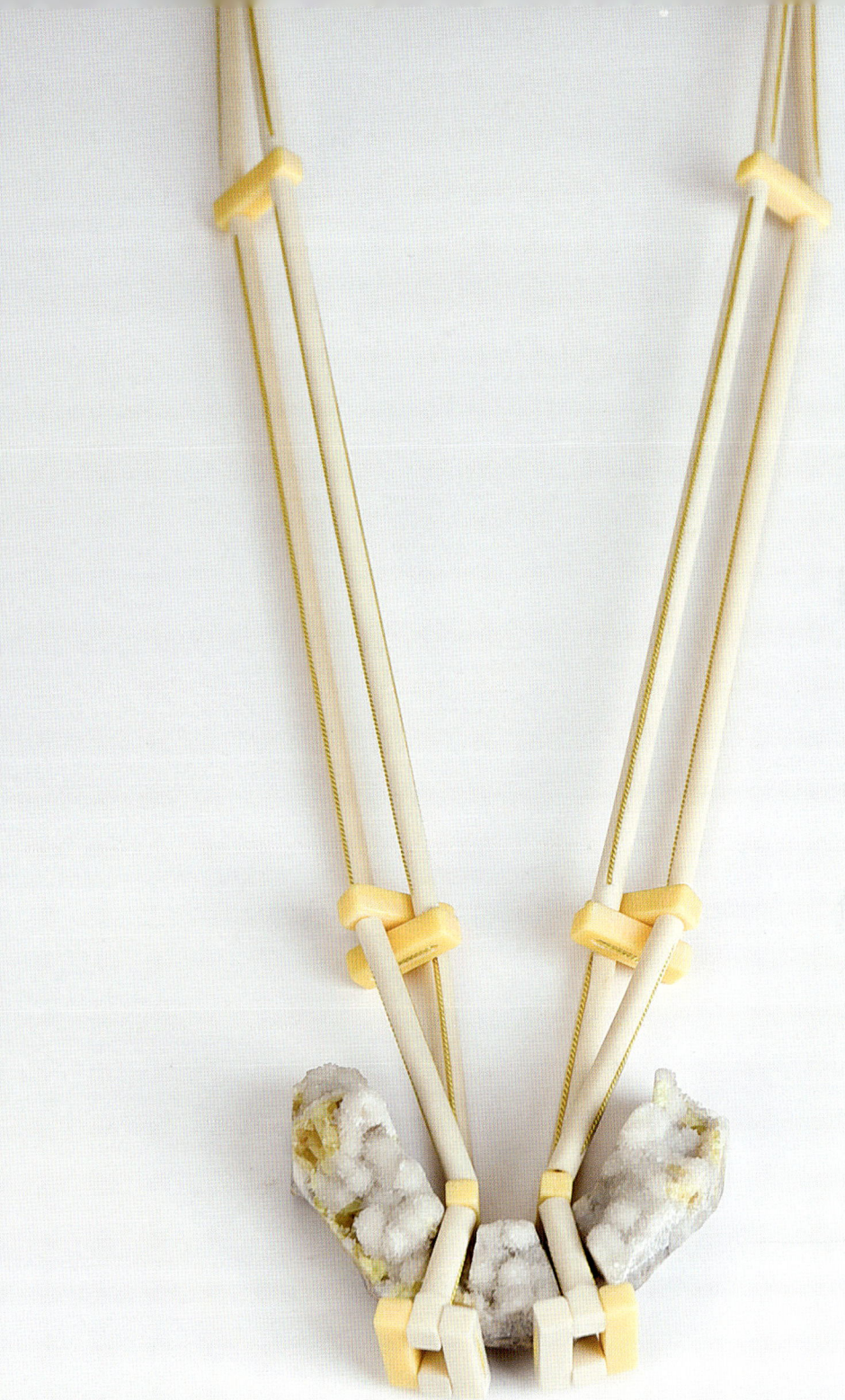

2010 „Hanging by a Thread I" Halsschmuck | *necklace*
Recon®, Seide, Cacholong | *Recon®, silk, cacholong*
Javier Moreno Frías, MA Graduation work

2010 Ohrhänger | *earrings*
Ebenholz, Polymer, Gold | *ebony, polymere, gold*
Brosche | *brooch*
Sheoakholz, Jaspis, Kit | *sheoak wood, jasper, kit*
Sachiyo Higaki, MA Graduation work

2010 Halsschmuck | *necklace*
Grenadill, Jaspis, Textil | *african blackwood, jasper, textile*
Sachiyo Higaki, MA Graduation work

2008 „Teller" Objekt | *object*
Keramik | *ceramic*
Julia Bocola, Diplom Graduation work

2008 „Kette Weiss" Halsschmuck | *necklace*
Cacholong | *cacholong*
Julia Bocola, Diplom Graduation work

2012 Studie | *study*
Kunststoff, Farbe | *plastic, paint*
Nina Fuchsberger, BFA Semester 4

2015 Objekt | *object*
Wolle, Holz, Stahl | *wool, wood, steel*
Maximilian Schröder, BFA Semester 1

2015 Objekt | *object*
Baumwolle, Gummi, Kunststoff, Stahl | *cotton, rubber, plastic, steel*
Maximilian Schröder, BFA Semester 3

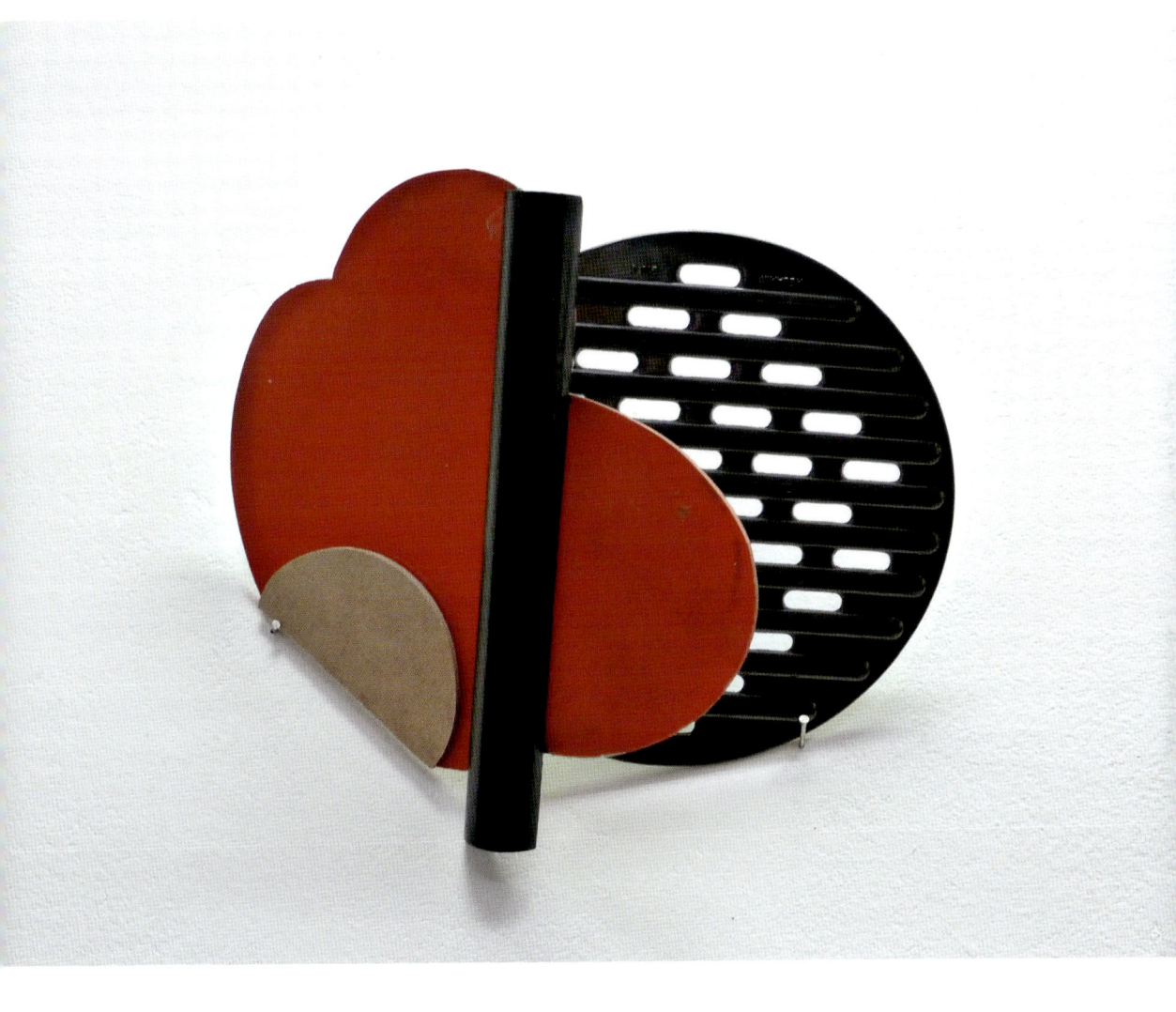

2013 Studie | *study*
Holz, Farbe | *wood, paint*
Julia Baudler, BA Semester 4

2015 „Trying to Feel what She Feels" Ohrhänger | *earrings*
Perle, Kunststoff, Silber | *pearl, plastic, silver*
„Constantly Beloved by…" Brosche | *brooch*
Glas, Kupfer, Stahl | *glass, copper, steel*
Elena Gorbunova, MFA Graduation work

2015 „Cuadrado" Brosche | *brooch*
Glasierte Keramik, Silber, Stahl | *glazed ceramic, silver, steel*
Elena Gorbunova, MFA Graduation work

2014 „Kontextschuh" Installation | *installation*
Schiefer, Eisen | *slate, iron*
Nina Fuchsberger, BFA Semester 5

2010 Fotomontage | *photomontage*
Alexander Friedrich, Diplom Semester 5

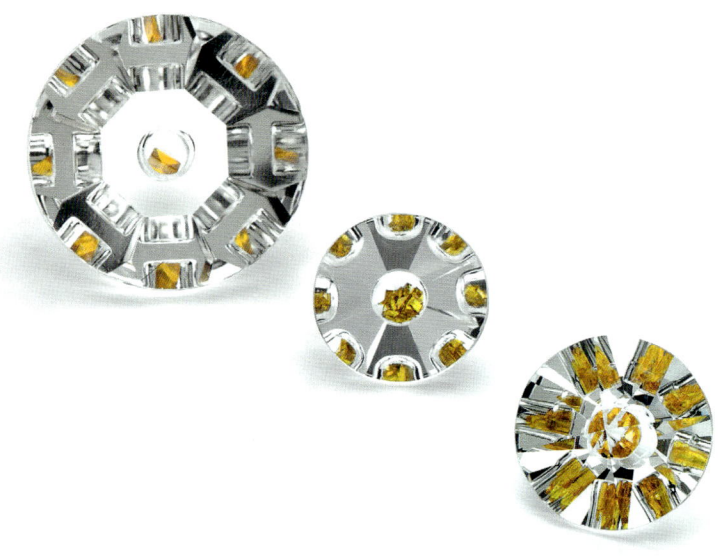

2012 Schliffe | *cuts*
Synthetischer Diamant, Bergkristall, | *synthetic diamond, rock crystal*
Alexander Friedrich, Diplom Semester 7

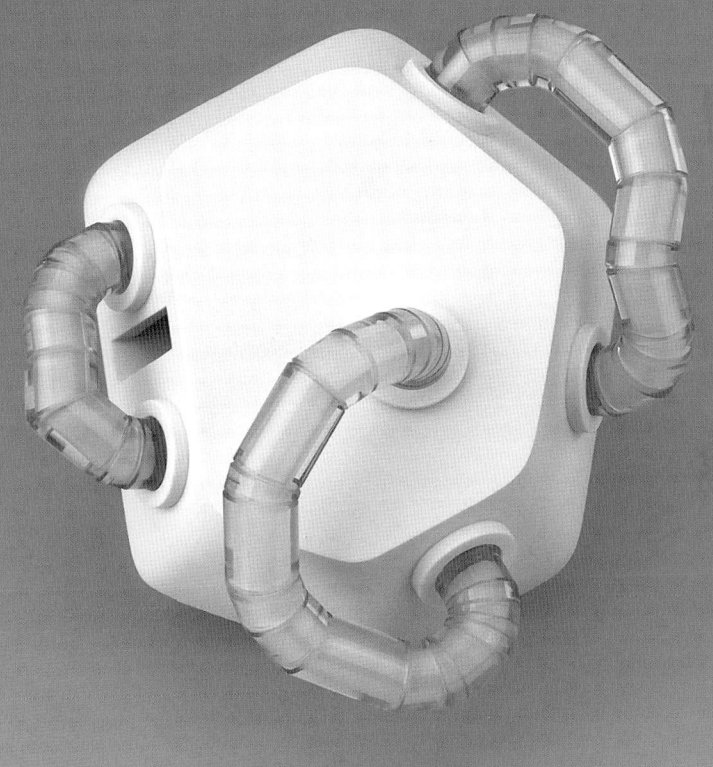

2012 Brosche | *brooch*
Bergkristall, Silber, Polystyrol, Lack | *rock crystal, silver, polystyrene, varnish*
Alexander Friedrich, Diplom Graduation work

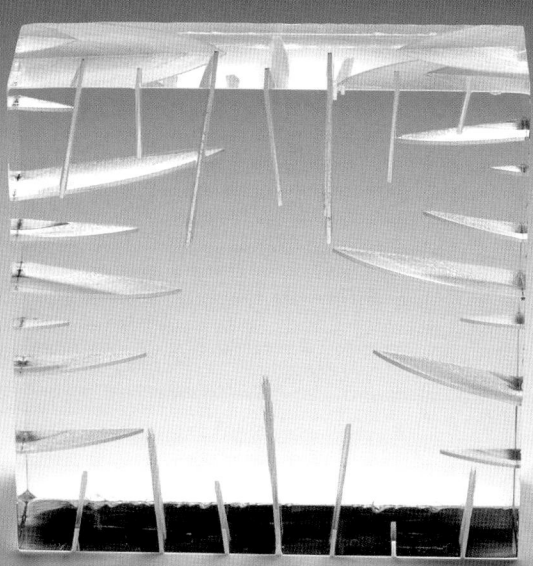

2009 Studien | *studies*
Acrylglas | *acrylic glass*
Diplom Semester 3

2012 Fotografie | *photography*
Rebekka Karg, BFA Semester 3

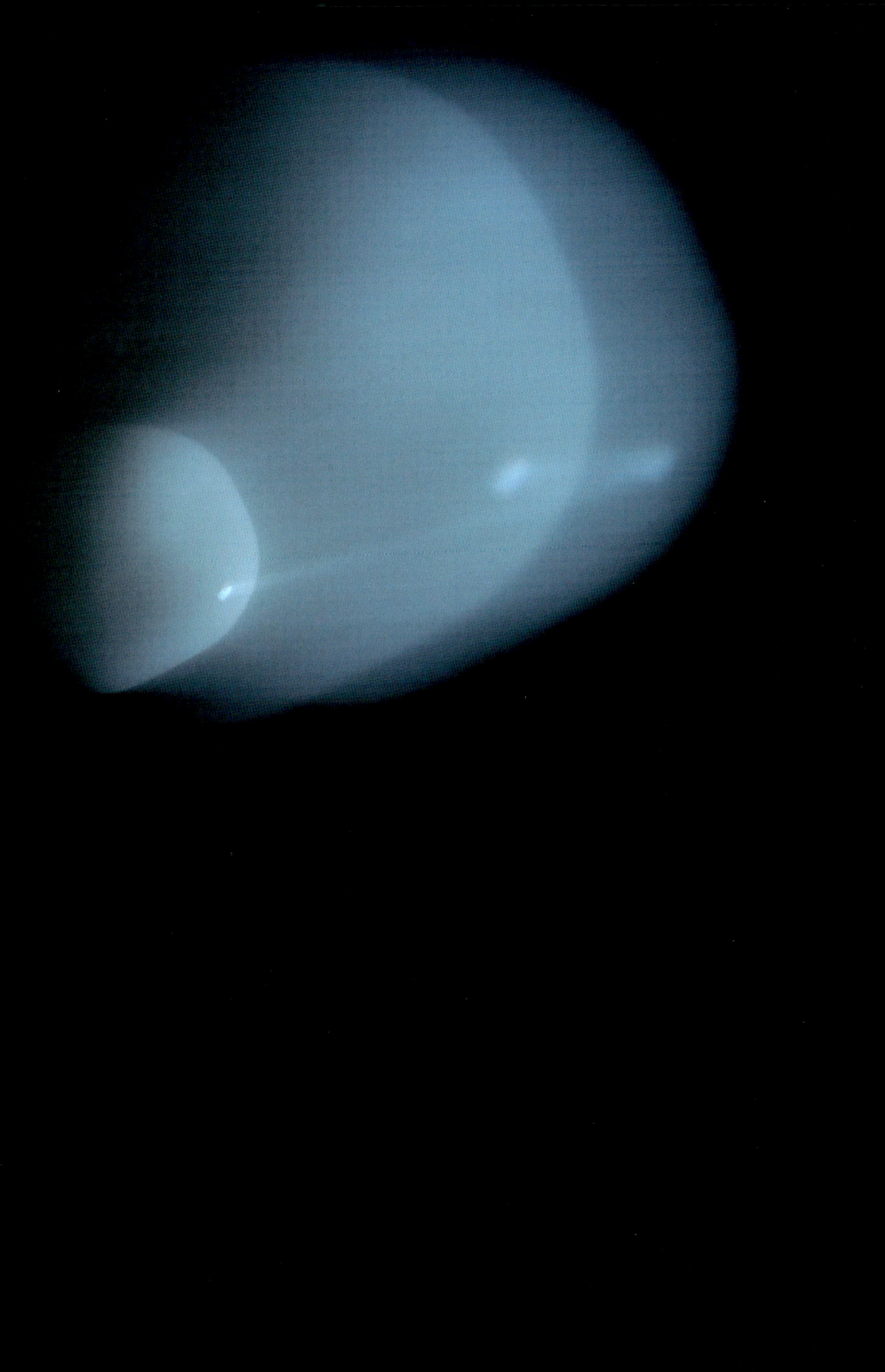

2014 „Venus Studies" Studien | *studies*
Arkansas, künstlicher Jaspis, Zirkon | *arkansas, artificial jasper, zircon*
Stahl, Achat | *steel, agate*
Typhaine Le Monnier, MFA Semester 3

2014 „Venus Studies" Studie | *study*
Aluminium, Farbe, Holz | *aluminium, paint, wood*
Typhaine Le Monnier, MFA Semester 3

2015 „Venus Studies" Halsschmuck | *necklaces*
Marmor, elastisches Band | *marble, elastic band*
Typhaine Le Monnier, MFA Graduation work

2013 Ohrhänger | *earrings*
Acrylglas, Silber, Achat | *acrylic glass, silver, agate*
Acrylglas, Silber, Bergkristall | *acrylic glass, silver, rock crystal*
Levan Jishkariani, BA Graduation work

2013 Ohrhänger | *earrings*
Acrylglas, Silber, Tigerauge | *acrylic glass, silver, tiger's eye*
Acrylglas, Silber, Chrysopras | *acrylic glass, silver, chrysoprase*
Levan Jishkariani, BA Graduation work

2007 „Dissonanz" Broschen | *brooches*
Papier, Stahl | *paper, steel*
Sun-Kyoung Kim, Diplom Graduation work

2007 „Dissonanz" Brosche | *brooch*
Achat, Latex, Silber, Stahl | *agate, latex, silver, steel*
Sun-Kyoung Kim, Diplom Graduation work

2009 Installation | *installation*
Wolle | *wool*
Sachiyo Higaki, MA Semster 3

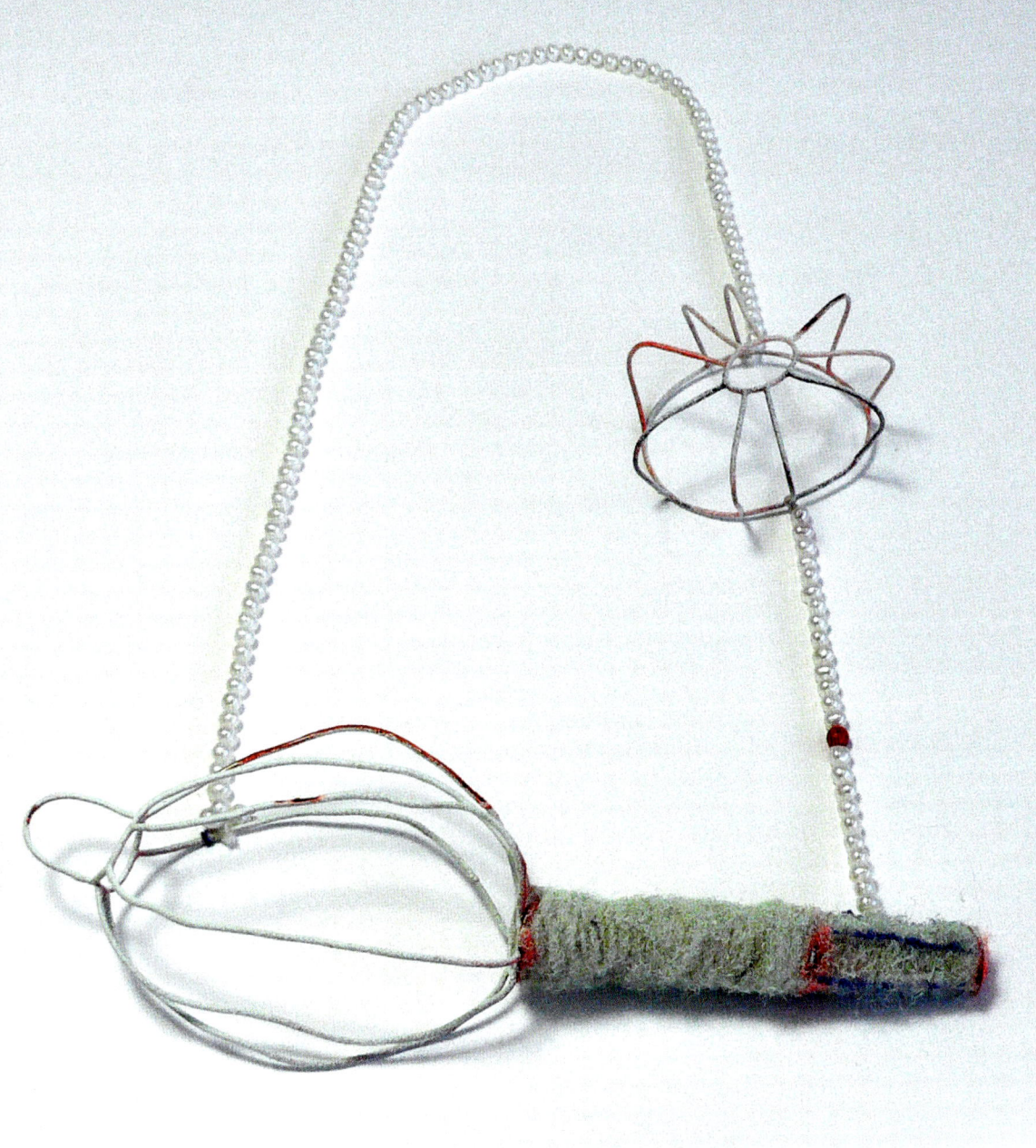

2011 „Cadavre Exquis 1" Halsschmuck | *necklace*
Neusilber, Wolle, Perlen, synthetische Koralle, Farbe | *new silver, wool, pearls, synthetic coral, paint*
Nelly Van Oost, MA Semester 3

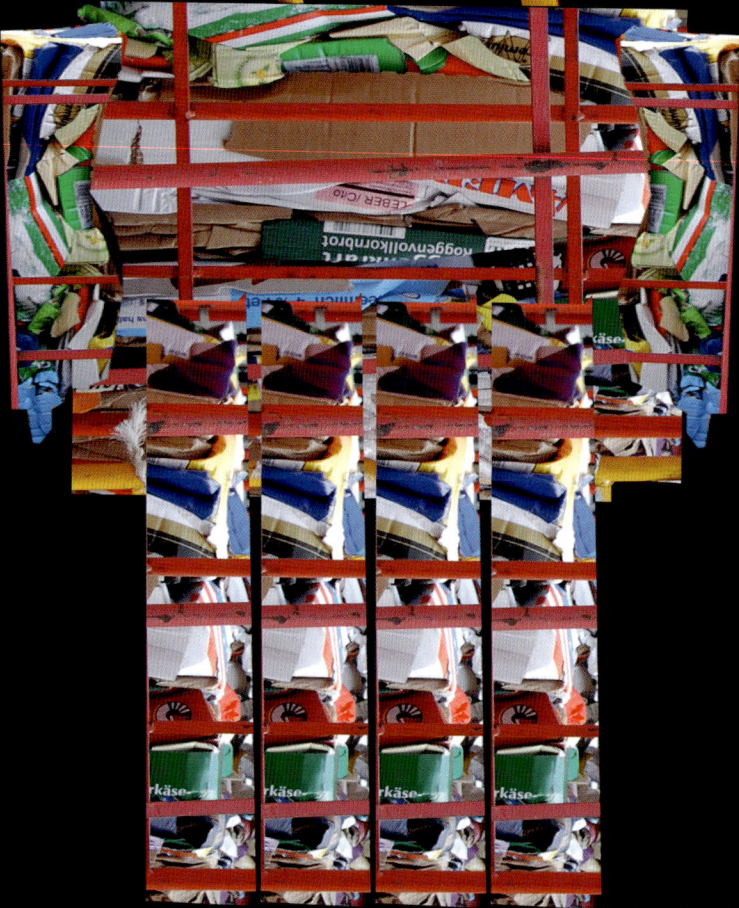

2014 „Schwebende Steine" Ohrringe | *earrings*
Achat, Edelstahl | *agate, stainless steel*
Petr Dvorak, MFA Graduation work

2015 „Muff" Halsschmuck | *necklace*
Baumwolle, Samt, Malachit, Rosenquarz, Sodalith, Amethyst, Schiefer, Onyx, Bergkristall
cotton, velvet, malachite, rose quartz, sodalite, amethyst, slate, onyx, rock crystal
Anna Jacobs, MFA Graduation work

2015 „Generationsgeschenk" Objekte | *objects*
Achat, Rauchquarz, Tigerauge, Labradorit | *agate, smoky quartz, tiger's eye, labradorite*
Anna Jacobs, MFA Graduation work

2016 Installation | *installation*
Spiegelschrank, Lippenstift, Fotografien | *mirror cabinet, lipstick, photographies*
Vanessa Zöller, BFA Semester 4

2016 Ringe | *rings*
geschwärztes Silber, Gold, Bergkristall, Fundstücke | *blackened silver, gold, rock crystal, found objects*
Amelie Spitz, MFA Semester 3

2016 „Lips" Fotografie | *photography*
Adriana Almeida Meza, MFA Semester 1

2016 „Schlagring" Ring | *ring*
Achat | *agate*
Lina Goltsios, BFA Semester 5

2016 Ring | *ring*
Bergkristall, Silber, Kunststoff | *rock crystal, silver, plastic*
Lina Goltsios, BFA Graduation work

2016 „Magic Mushrooms" Objekte | *objects*
Heißkleber, Textil, Papier, Schaumstoff, Draht, Holz, Glas | *hot glue, textile, paper, foamed material, wire, wood, glass*
Rinke Wassenberg, BFA Semester 4

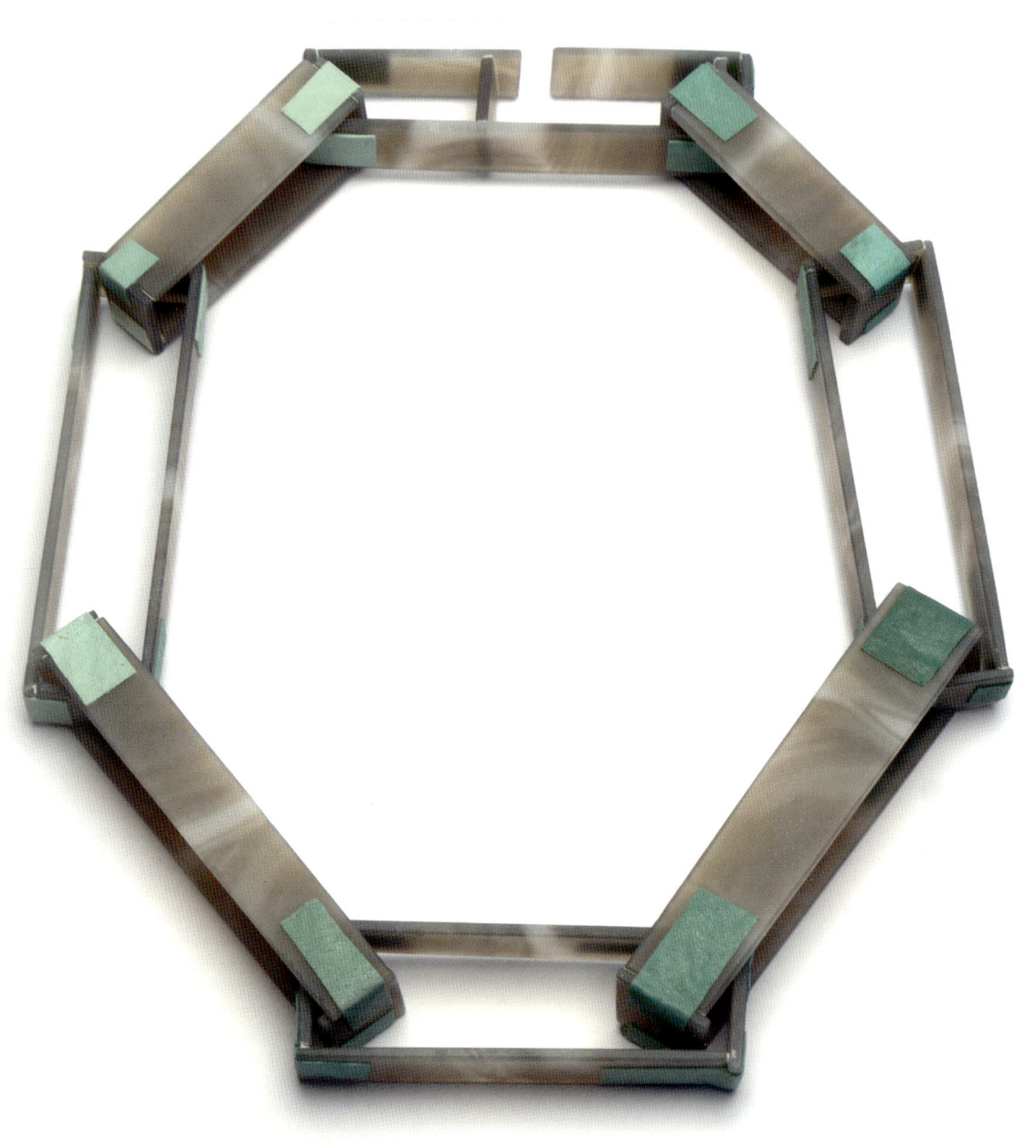

2016 „Come around" Halsschmuck | *necklace*
Achat, Gießharz, Pigment | *agate, resin, pigment*
Julia Obermaier, BFA Graduation work

2016 „Round the corner" Brosche | *brooch*
Achat, Gießharz, Pigment, Edelstahl | *agate, resin, pigment, stainless steel*
Julia Obermaier, BFA Graduation work

2015 „Black with Black " Brosche | *brooch*
Hanji, Reis, Ebenholz, geschwärztes Silber, Firnis, Obsidian | *hanji, rice, ebony, blackened silver, lacquer, obsidian*
Saerom Kong, MFA Graduation work

2015 Broschen | *brooches*
Hanji, Bohnen, Messing, Farbe | *hanji, beans, brass, paint*
Hanji, Reis, Bohnen, Silber, Holz, Farbe | *hanji, rice, beans, silver, wood, paint*
Saerom Kong, MFA Graduation work

2011 Ohrhänger | *earrings*
Achat, Silber | *agate, silver*
Pia Sommerlad, BA Graduation work

2014 „Black'n'White" Brosche | *brooch*
Silber, Gießharz, Stahl | *silver, resin, steel*
Julia Baudler, BA Graduation work

2012 „Brosche für Peter der Bär" Brosche | *brooch*
Silber, vergoldetes Kupfer, Glas, Lack | *silver, gilded copper, glass, varnish*
Anna Ameling, MA Graduation work

2007 Edelsteinobjekte | *gemstone objects*
Zirkonia | *zirconia*
Katharina Vanselow, Diplom Graduation work

2014 „The Cut" Brosche | *brooch*
Muschelschale, Pyrit, Harz, Silber | *mussel shell, pyrite, resin, silver*
Cristina Martí Mató, MFA Graduation work

2014 „ME" Brosche | *brooch*
Achat, Muschelschale, Bergkristall, Harz, Jaspis, Silber, Messing, Kupfer
agate, mussel shell, rock crystal, resin, jasper, silver, brass, copper
Cristina Martí Mató, MFA Graduation work

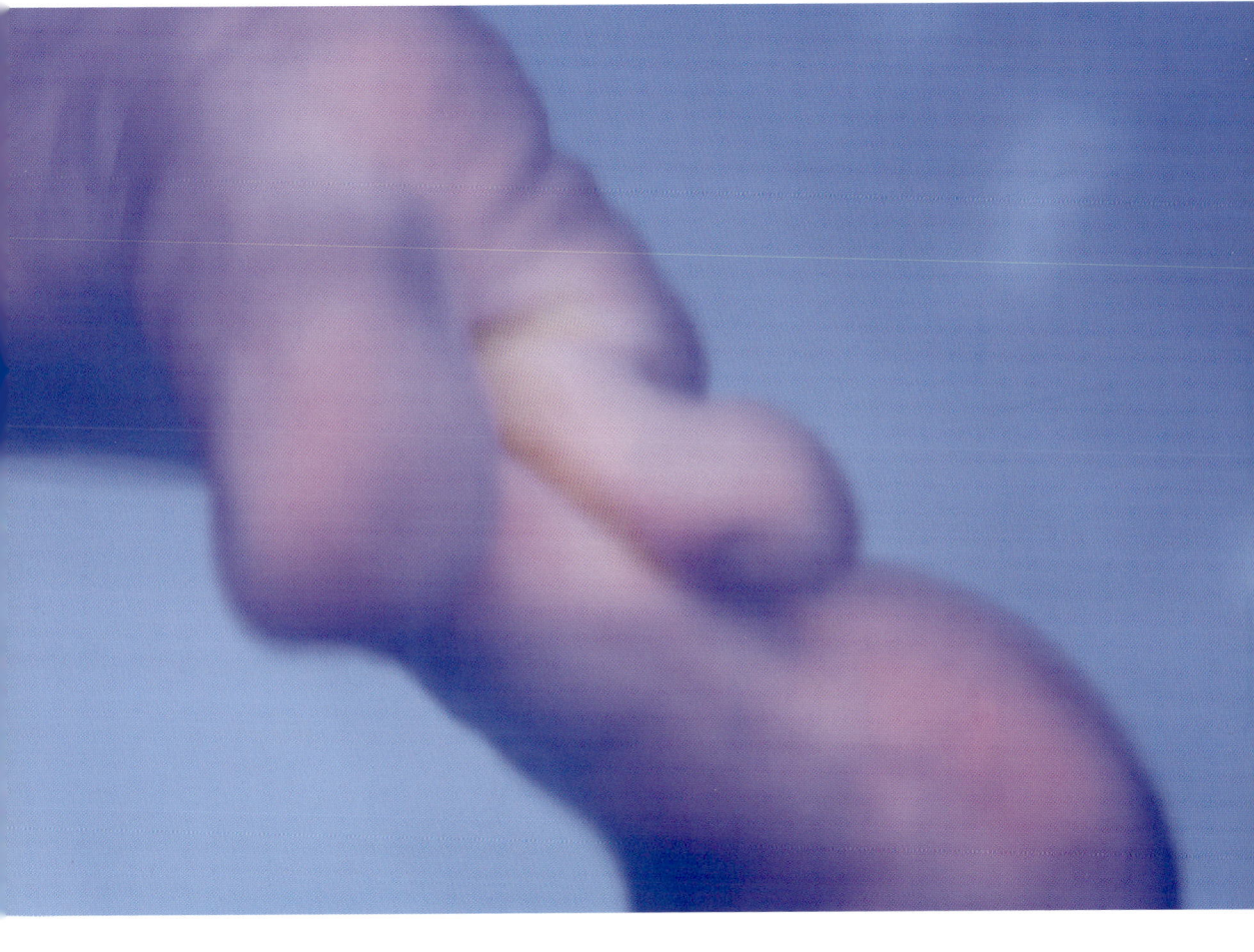

2013 Kopfschmuck | *headpiece*
Leder, Stoff | *leather, fabric*
Sari Räthel, BFA Graduation work

2013 Halsschmuck | *necklace*
Achat, Leder, Edelstahl | *agate, leather, stainless steel*
Sari Räthel, BFA Graduation work

2011 Studie | *study*
Achat, PVC, Neopren | *agate, PVC, neoprene*
Sari Räthel, BFA Semester 3

2009 „Sperrmüll" Fotomontage | *photomontage*
Tatiana Giorgadse, Diplom Semester 2

2010 Fotomontage | *photomontage*
Tatjana Giorgadse, Diplom Semester 4

2012 „Never Was the Moon" Brosche | *brooch*
Achat, Stein aus dem Fluss Rioni, Silber | *agate, river Rioni stone, silver*
Tatjana Giorgadse, Diplom Graduation work

2012 „Achatia" Ohrhänger | *earrings*
Achat, Silber, Silikon | *agate, silver, silicone*
Tatjana Giorgadse, Diplom Graduation work

2010 Fotomontage | *photomontage*
Tatjana Giorgadse, Diplom Semester 4

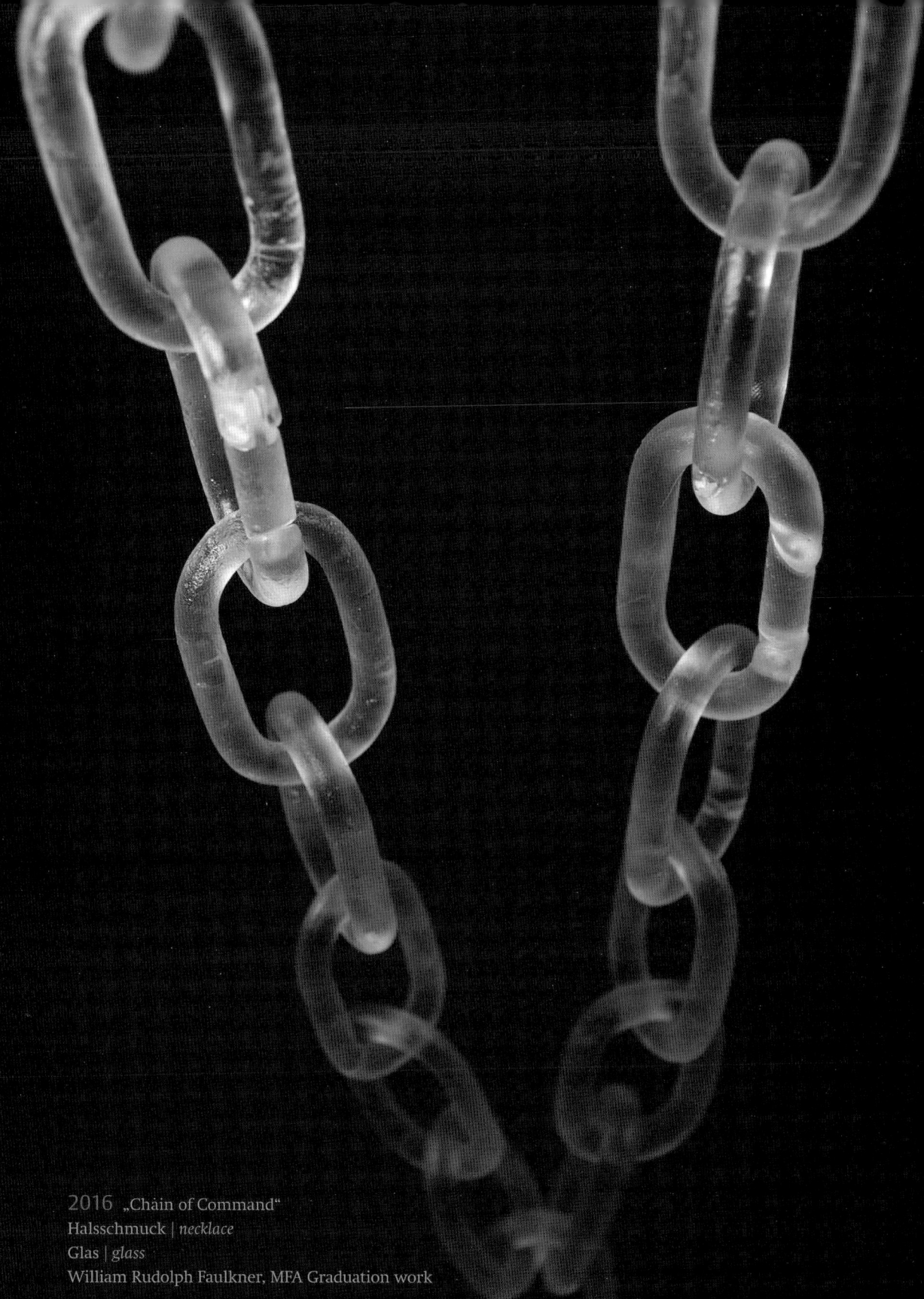

2016 „Chain of Command"
Halsschmuck | *necklace*
Glas | *glass*
William Rudolph Faulkner, MFA Graduation work

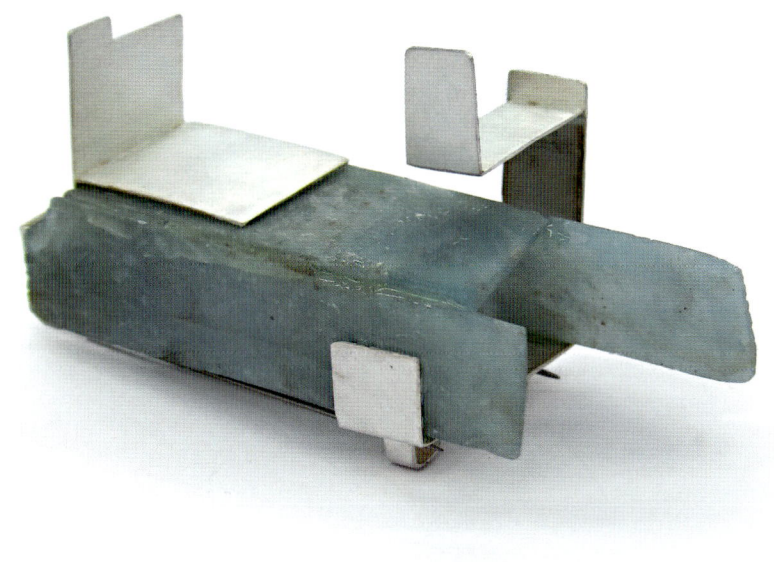

2011 „Nowhere in between VIII" Brosche | *brooch*
Silber, Aquamarin | *silver, aquamarine*
Estela Saez Vilanova, MA Graduation work

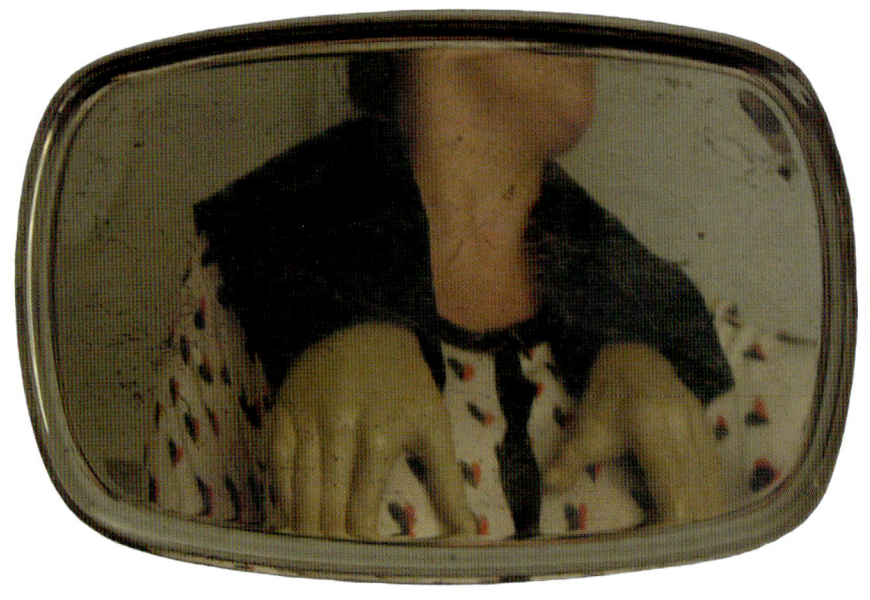

2013 „Der Grabscher" Halsschmuck | *necklace*
Textil, Kunststoff | *textile, plastic*
Katja Köditz, BA Graduation work

2013 „Zwangsjacke" Jacke | *jacket*
Gobelin | *gobelin*
Katja Köditz, BA Graduation work

2015 „Call the Professor" Video still | *video still*
Katja Köditz, MFA Graduation work

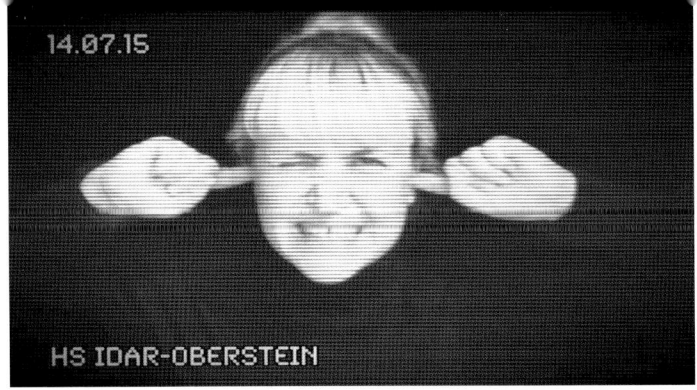
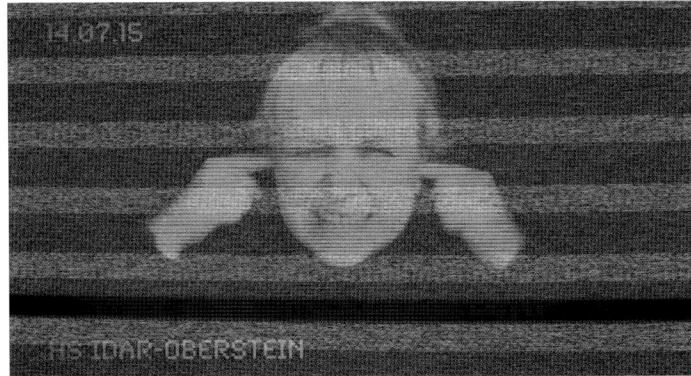

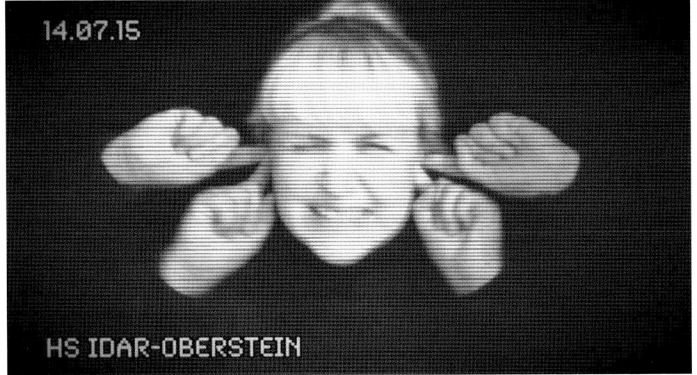

2015 „At Night in School" Video still | *video still*
Katja Köditz, MFA Graduation work

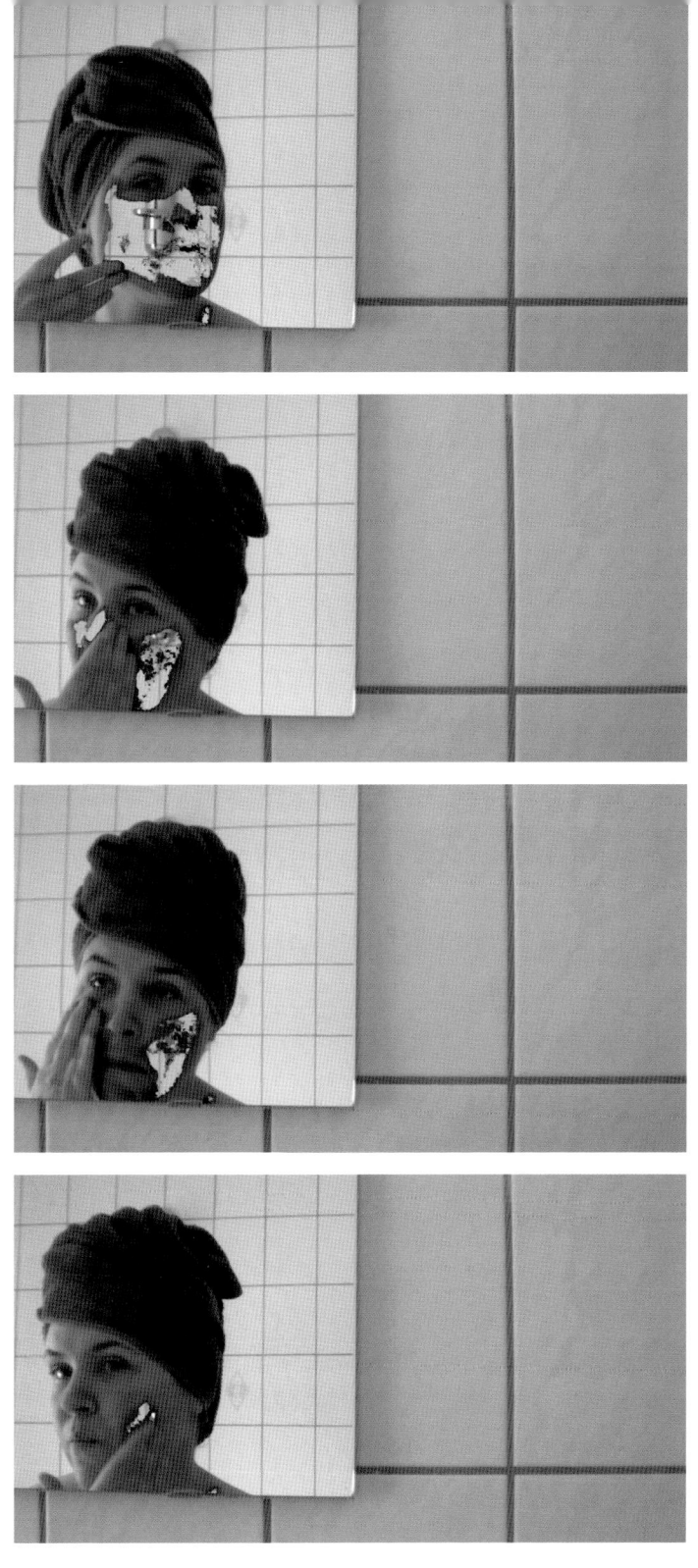

2015 „Ich existiere" Video still | *video still*
Katja Köditz, MFA Graduation work

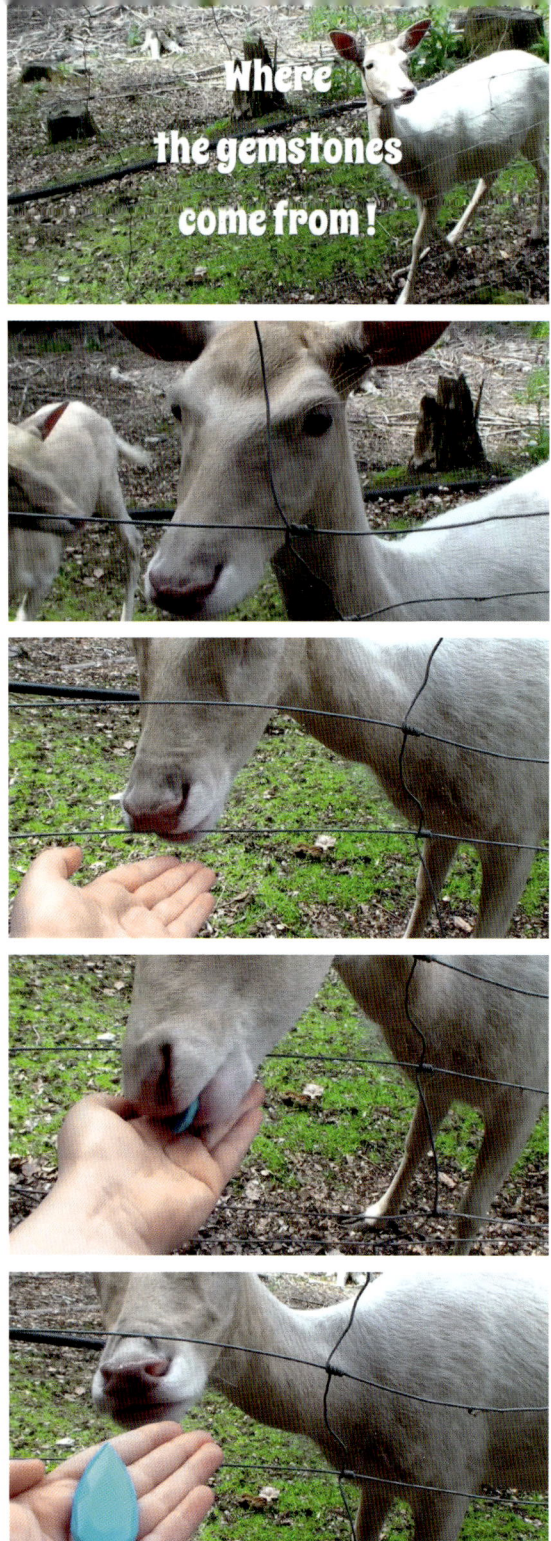

2015 „Where the gemstones come from" Video still | *video still*
Katja Köditz, MFA Graduation work

2014 Objekt | *object*
Kunststoff, Achat | *plastic, agate*
Nina Fuchsberger, BFA Semester 5

2008 Studie | *study*
Keramik, Textil | *ceramic, textile*
Francisca Bauzá, Diplom Semester 4

2010 „patrón II" Halsschmuck | *necklace*
Kupfer, Emaille, Silber | *copper, enamel, silver*
Francisca Bauzá, Diplom Graduation work

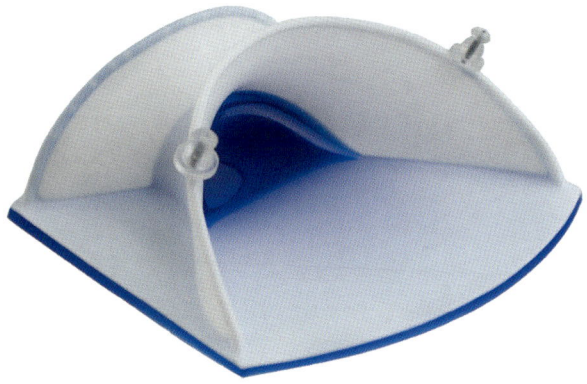

2010 Broschen | *brooches*
Polystyrol, Harz, Edelstahl | *polystyrene, resin, stainless steel*
Silke Rehermann, Diplom Graduation work

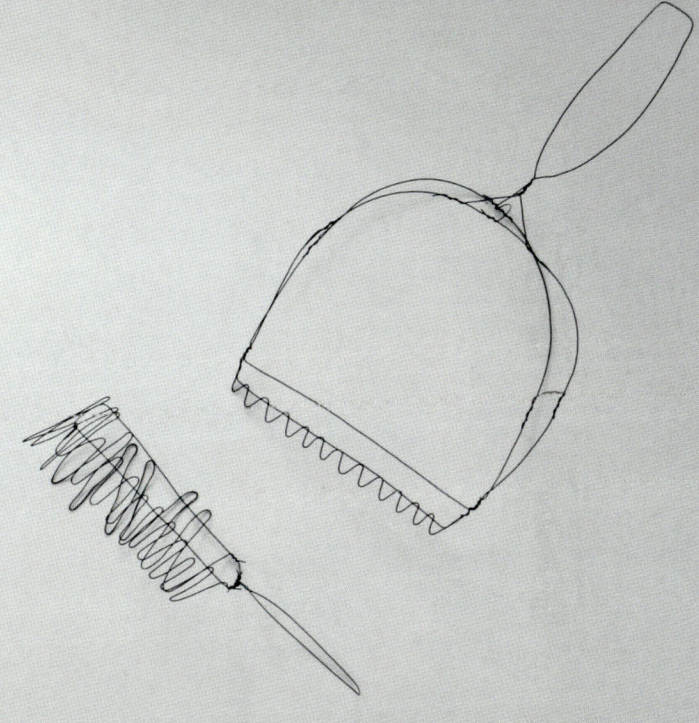

2007 „Kehre und Schaufel" Objekt | *object*
Eisen | *iron*
Silke Rehermann, Diplom Semester 3

2014 „Leopard" Halsschmuck | *necklace*
Emaille, Kupfer, Silber, Gold | *enamel, copper, silver, gold*
Tabea Reulecke, MFA Semester 3

2006 „Kissing Elephants" Brosche | *brooch*
Emaille, Kupfer, Gold | *enamel, copper, gold*
Tabea Reulecke, Diplom Graduation work

2006 „So Close To" Brosche | *brooch*
Emaille, Kupfer, Silber, Knochen | *enamel, copper, silver, bone*
Tabea Reulecke, Diplom Graduation work

2011 „Holz Haus" Halsschmuck | *necklace*
Holz, Silber | *wood, silver*
Sabine Conrad, Diplom Graduation work

2012 Brosche | *brooch*
Achat, Silber, Poxipol® | *agate, silver, Poxipol®*
Penka Arabova, Diplom Graduation work

2012 Brosche | *brooch*
Achat, Silber, Kuhhorn, Poxipol® | *agate, silver, cow horn, Poxipol®*
Penka Arabova, Diplom Graduation work

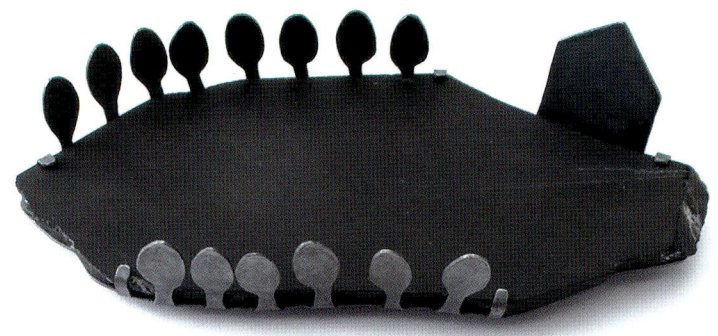

2010 „Seebrosche I" Brosche | *brooch*
Onyx, Silber, Stahl | *onyx, silver, steel*
Deborah Rudolph, Diplom Graduation work

2010 „Ohne Farbe" Halsschmuck | *necklace*
Jade, Achat, Jaspis, Kiesel, Silber, Kevlar® | *jade, agate, jasper, pebble, silver, Kevlar®*
Deborah Rudolph, Diplom Graduation work

2008 Halsschmuck | *necklace*
Emaille, Kupfer | *enamel, copper*
Danni Schwaag, Diplom Graduation work

2008 Brosche | *brooch*
Emaille, Kupfer, Perlmutt, Gold | *enamel, copper, mother of pearl, gold*
Danni Schwaag, Diplom Graduation work

2007 „Grau" Brosche | *brooch*
Rohseide, Gold | *raw silk, gold*
SunHi Jäger, Diplom Graduation work

2016 „5:13" Fotografie | *photography*
Jiun-You Ou, MFA Semester 1

2014 „Hängende Häuser" Fotografie | *photography*
Carolin Denter, BFA Semester 1

2013 Studien | *studies*
Holz, Farbe | *wood, paint*
Daniela Malev, MFA Semester 3

2011 „Wer Seid Das Ihr" Installation | *installation*
Diverse Materialien | *mixed materials*
Nils Schmalenbach, BA Graduation work

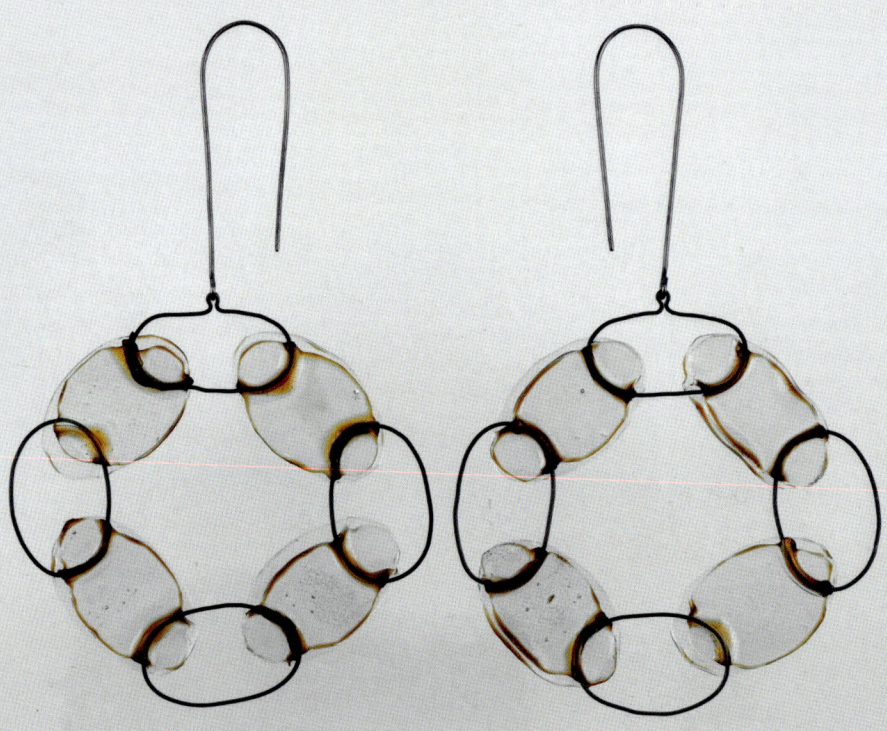

2007 „Jetzt und danach – eins greift ins andere – immerzu" Ohrringe | *earrings*
Eisen, PVC, Silber | *iron, PVC, silver*
Susanne Kaube, Diplom Graduation work

2010 Broschen | *brooches*
eloxiertes Aluminium, Reflektor, Stahl | *anodized aluminium, cat's eye, steel*
Marcella Ferretti, Diplom Graduation work

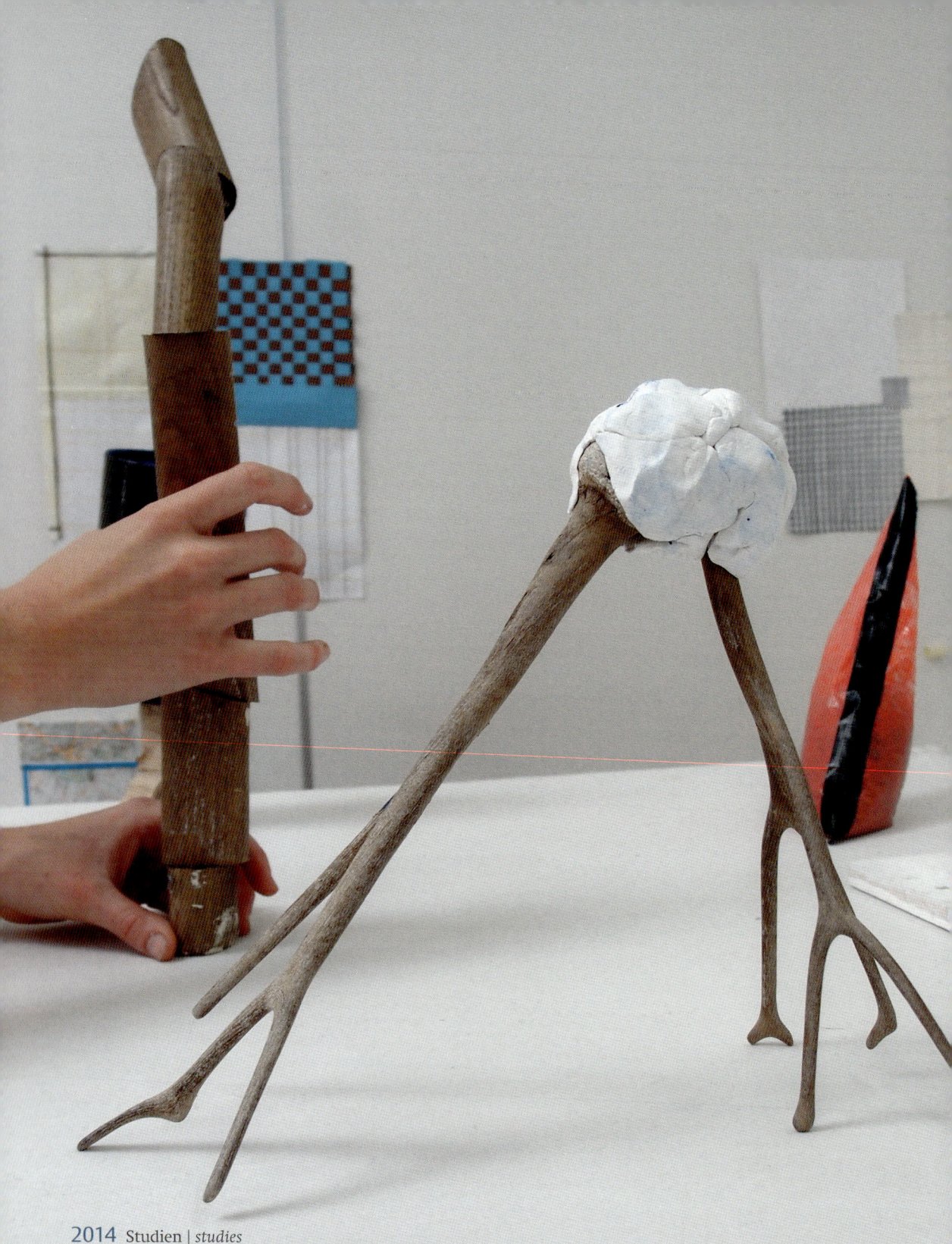

2014 Studien | *studies*
Diverse Materialien | *mixed materials*
Pia Groh, BFA Semester 2

2016 Brosche | brooch
Silber, teilweise geschwärzt, Farbe, Stahl | partly blackened silver, paint, steel
Ferràn Iglesias Barón, MFA Graduation work

2016 „Tatzia 11" Halsschmuck | *necklace*
Porzellan, Silber, Pigment | *porcelain, silver, pigment*
Gabriela Cohn, MFA Graduation work

2009 Brosche | *brooch*
Kunststoff, Silber, Stahl | *plastic, silver, steel*
Ulrike Kraus, Diplom Graduation work

2014 „Walk of Fame" Ring | *ring*
Silber, Turmalin | *silver, tourmaline*
Héctor Lasso, MFA Semester 2

2013 „Dicker als Wasser" Halsschmuck | *necklace*
Glas, Stahl | *glass, steel*
Katharina Reimann, BA Graduation work

2012 Installation | *installation*
Nylonstrümpfe, Stahl | *nylons, steel*
Katharina Reimann, BA Semester 3

2014 Ohrringe | *earrings*
Gießharz, Kaffeepad, Silber, Eisen | *resin, coffee pad, silver, iron*
Sharareh Aghaei, BFA Graduation work

2014 Halsschmuck | *necklace*
Gießharz, Fotografie, Textil, Silber | *resin, photography, textile, silver*
Sharareh Aghaei, BFA Graduation work

2015 „Boris spielt Risiko" Objekt | *object*
Silber, Kunststoff, Granat | *silver, plastic, garnet*
Christina Erlacher, BA Graduation work

2015 „Klaus versenkt Schiffe" Fotografie | photography
Christina Erlacher, BA Graduation work

2011 „Imaginarium X" Kopfhörer | *headphones*
Leder, Metall, Elektronik | *leather, metal, electronics*
Karina Mihalus, Diplom Graduation work

2011 „Perfekt Kristallin III + IV + V" Broschen | *brooches*
Schieferfurnier, Magnete, Stahl, Flock | *slate veneer, magnets, steel, flock*
Antje Stolz, Diplom Graduation work

2015 „Being on the Fig Tree" Halsschmuck | *necklace*
Zitronenchrysopras, Kevlar®, Kunststoff, Olivenholz, Firnis | *lemon chrysoprase, Kevlar®, plastic, olive wood, lacquer*
Ignasi Cavaller, MFA Graduation work

2015 „Mixing Eggs with Snails" Halsschmuck | *necklace*
Landschaftsjaspis, Kevlar®, Messing, Firnis | *landscape jasper, Kevlar®, brass, lacquer*
„Is Like an Oil Puddle" Brosche | *brooch*
Silber, Stahl, Kalkstein, Zitronenchrysopras | *silver, steel, limestone, lemon chrysoprase*
Ignasi Cavaller, MFA Graduation work

2013 „Duality" Halsschmuck | *necklace*
Recon®, Garn | *Recon®, thread*
Patrícia Domingues, MA Graduation work

2013 „Duality" Halsschmuck | *necklace*
Recon®, Garn | *Recon®, thread*
Patrícia Domingues, MA Graduation work

2011 Studie | *study*
Recon®, Gips | *Recon®, plaster*
Patrícia Domingues, MA Semester 2

2012 Studie | *study*
Recon® | *Recon®*
Patrícia Domingues, MA Semester 3

2014 Studie | *study*
Karton, Farbe | *cardboard, paint*
Salla Lahtinen, Exchange Student Saimaa University Finland

2014 Ringe | *rings*
Hämatit, Achat, Stein | *hematite, agate, stone*
Hämatit | *hematite*
Elvira Golombosi, MFA Graduation work

2008 Fotomontage | *photomontage*
Anne Wiedau, Diplom Semester 2

2011 „Car(bon)_Hybrid" Halsschmuck | *necklace*
Recon®, Karbon, Quarz, Gummi | *Recon®, carbon, quartz, rubber*
Anne Wiedau, Diplom Graduation work

2011 Halsschmuck | *necklace*
Stahl | *steel*
Kim Friederich, Diplom Graduation work

2011 Schliffe | *cuts*
Synthetischer Spinell | *synthetic spinel*
Mirjam Dreher, Diplom Graduation work

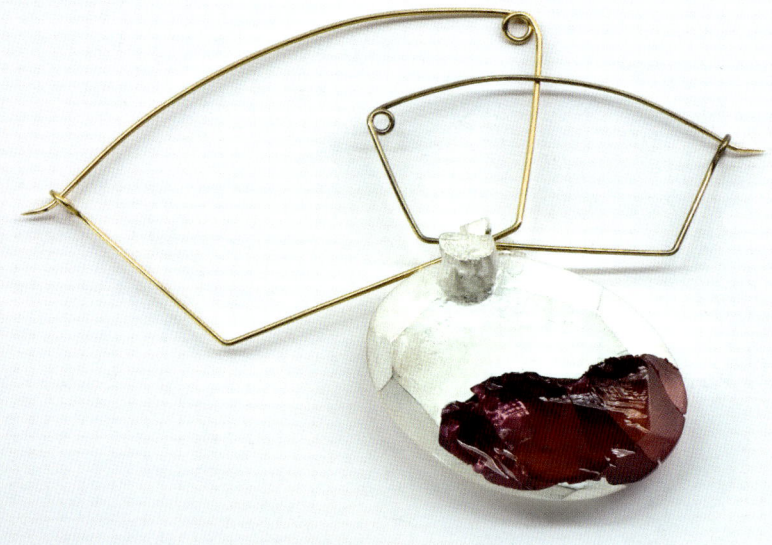

2009 „mADhOUSE 18" Brosche | *brooch*
Synthetischer Rubin, Silber, Gold | *synthetic ruby, silver, gold*
Taehee In, Diplom Graduation work

2009 „mADhOUSE 13" Brosche | *brooch*
Achat, Silber | *agate, silver*
„mADhOUSE 24" Ring | *ring*
Silber, Rauchquarz | *silver, smoky quartz*
Taehee In, Diplom Graduation work

2014 „Lluvina" Brosche | *brooch*
Kiesel, Silber, Gießharz, Kunststoff | *pebble, silver, resin, plastic*
Alejandra Solar, MFA Graduation work

2014 „Comala" Halsschmuck | *necklace*
Kiesel, Silber | *pebble, silver*
Alejandra Solar, MFA Graduation work

2015 „Emotions" Broschen | *brooches*
Holzkohle, Holz, Lack | *charcoal, wood, varnish*
Denise Ebert, BFA Semester 4

2014 „QR-code" Brosche | *brooch*
Achat, Silber, Edelstahl | *agate, silver, stainless steel*
Pia Groh, BFA Semester 3

2016 „1°" Halsschmuck | *necklace*
Gold, Achat | *gold, agate*
Pia Groh, BFA Semester 5

2016 „2°" Halsschmuck | *necklace*
Achat, Silber | *agate, silver*
Pia Groh, BFA Semester 5

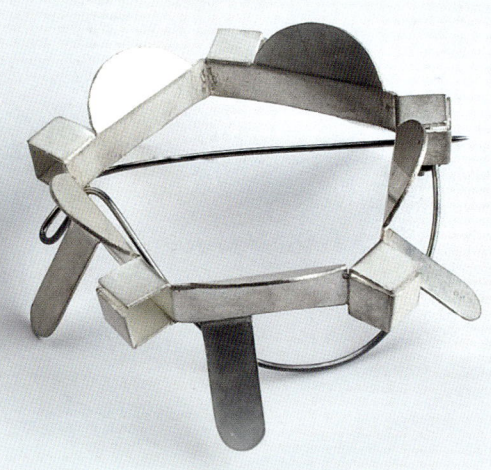

2011 „H(a)unting Truth" Broschen | *brooches*
Silber, Edelstahl | *silver, stainless steel*
versilbertes, teilweise geschwärztes Kupfer, Recon®, Stahl | *blackened silver plated copper, Recon®, steel*
Barbora Dzuráková, MA Graduation work

2009 Fotomontage | *photomontage*
Hye-Shil Kim, Diplom Semester 2

2014 Objekt | *object*
Baumwolle, Stahl | *cotton, steel*
Rinke Wassenberg, BFA Semester 1

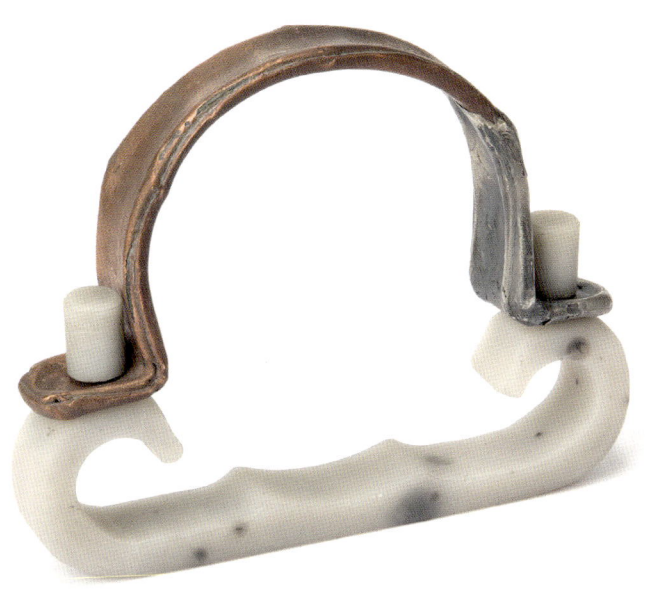

2015 „Armlink 4+6" Armreifen | *bracelets*
rotvergoldetes Kupfer, Tigerauge | *red gold plated copper, tiger's eye*
geschwärztes Kupfer, Arkansas | *blackened copper, arkansas*
Dana Seachuga, MFA Graduation work

2015 Objekt | *object*
Schiefer, Farbe | *slate, paint*
Qi Wang, MFA Semester 3

2016 „Puzzle Ring" Ring | *ring*
Bergkristall | *rock crystal*
Qi Wang, MFA Semester 3

2015 „Adrenalin kickt IO" Fotografie | *photography*
Vanessa Zöller, BFA Semester 1

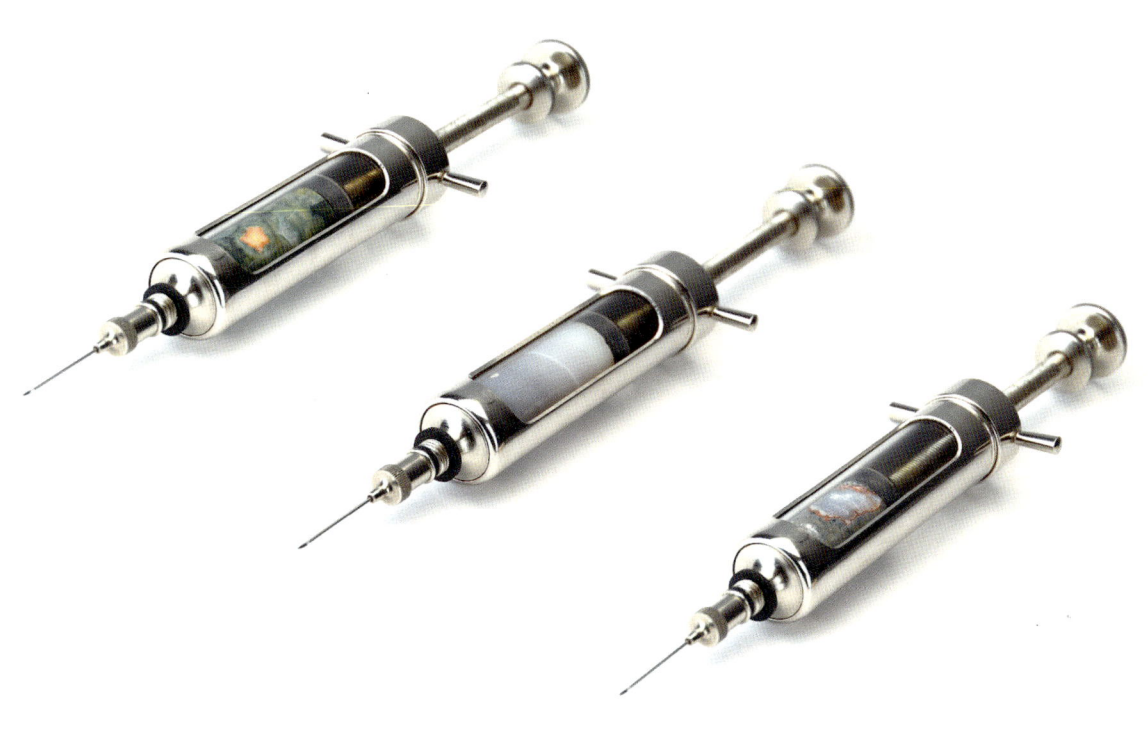

2016 Objekte | *objects*
Spritze, Jaspis, Achat | *syringe, jasper, agate*
Qi Wang, MFA Semester 3

2015 „Möpse" Fotografie | *photography*
Maximilian Schröder, BFA Semester 3

2016 Objekte | *objects*
Marmor | *marble*
Katie Jayne Britchford, MFA Semester 2

2009 „Kleines Schwarzes mit Perlenkette" Kleid | *dress*
Textil, Edelstahl | *textile, stainless steel*
Francisca Bauzá, Diplom Graduation work

2014 "Fields of Miesau" Fotografie | *photography*
William Rudolph Faulkner, MFA Semester 1

2013 Foto/Halsschmuck | *photo/necklace*
Dagmar Dluzniak, BA Graduation work

2011 Brosche | *brooch*
Silber, Wachs, Kunstharz, Aquamarin | *silver, wax, epoxy resin, aquamarine*
Lisa Kröber, Diplom Graduation work

2016 „What Is Behind" Brosche | *brooch*
MDF, Farbe, Papier | *MDF, paint, paper*
Sabine Flexer, MFA Semester 2

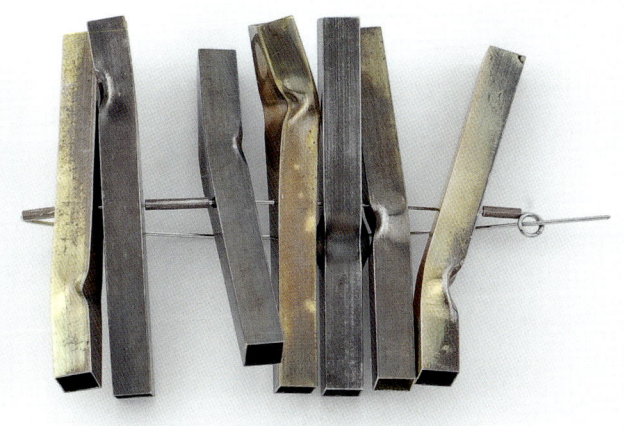

2008 Brosche | *brooch*
Silber, Stahl | *silver, steel*
Frauke Grosch, Diplom Graduation work

2016 „reMake Onno Boekhoudt" Studie | *study*
Diverse Materialien | *mixed materials*
Gina-Nadine Müller, BFA Semester 1

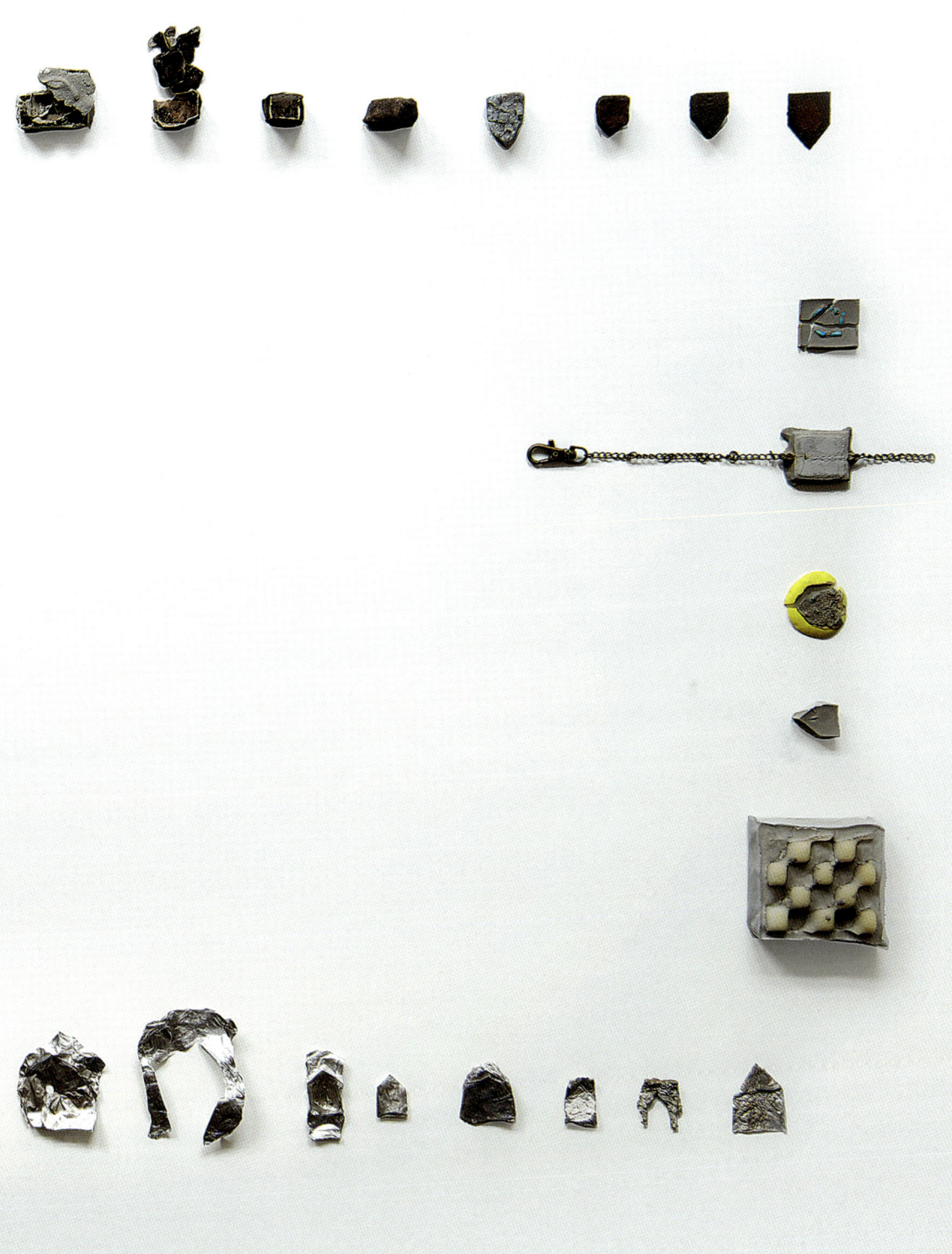

2010 Fotomontage | *photomontage*
Hye-Shil Kim, Diplom Semester 5

2015 „La cabane" Video still | *video still*
Katja Köditz, MFA Semester 3

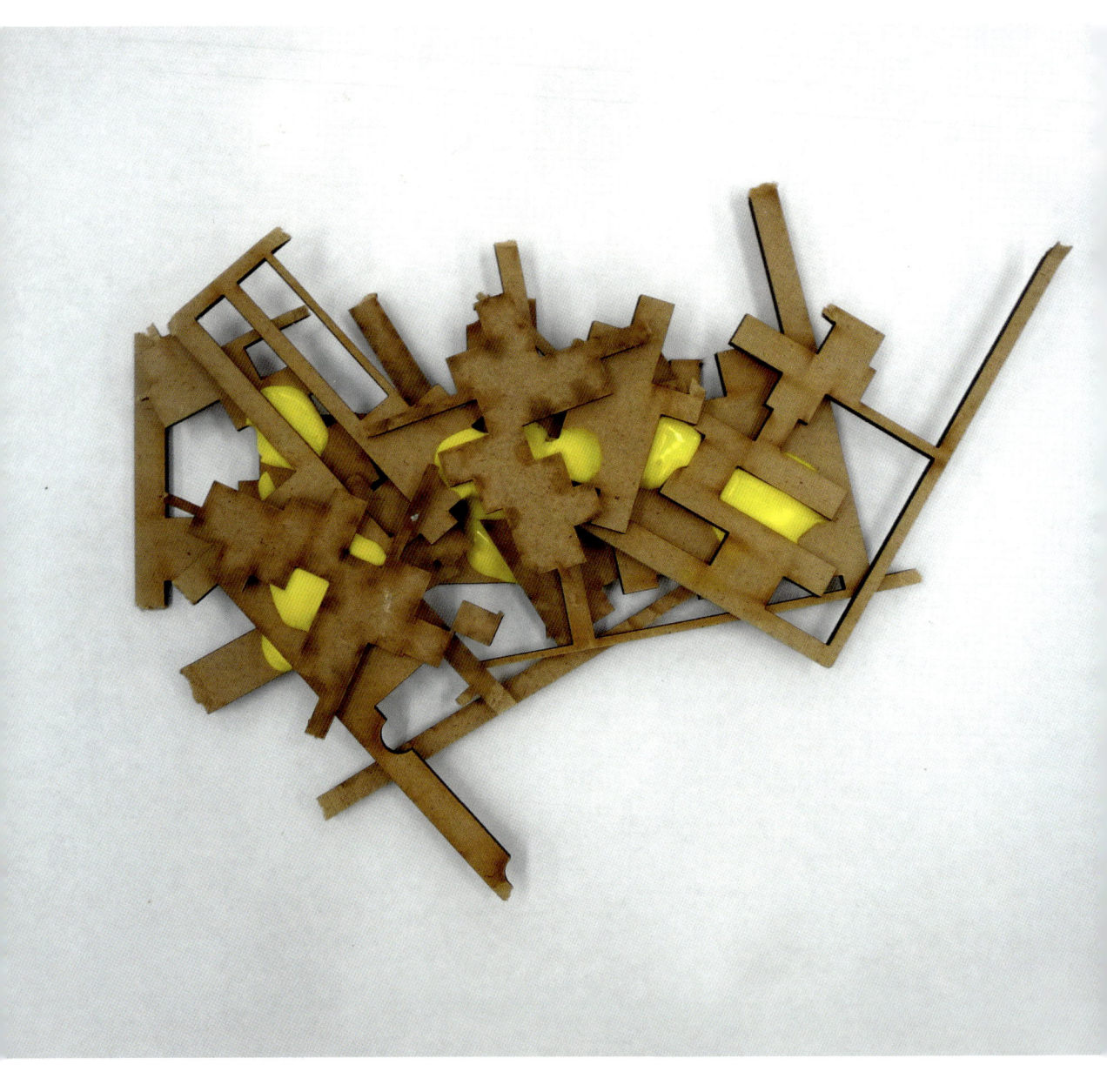

2013 Studie | *study*
Hartfaserplatte, Klebstoff, Pigment | *hardboard, glue, pigment*
Kathrin Münsch, BA Semester 4

2015 „Das Autito" Brosche | *brooch*
Holz, Cacholong, Papier, Farbe, Stahl | *wood, cacholong, paper, paint, steel*
Eva Burton, MFA Semester 2

2016 Objekt | object
Achat | agate
John Maddox, BFA Semester 1

2006 „Facetten: Brilliant und Triangel" Broschen | *brooches*
Edelstahl | *stainless steel*
Eva Röhrig, Diplom Graduation work

2016 Halsschmuck | *necklace*
Marmor, Harz mit Graphit, Textil | marble, resin with graphite, textile
Catalina Brenes, MFA Graduation work

2016 Broschen | *brooches*
Marmor, Silber, Harz mit Graphit, Edelstahl | *marble, silver, resin with graphite, stainless steel*
Catalina Brenes, MFA Graduation work

2007 „Königsring" Ring | *ring*
Silber, Rauchquarz | *silver, smoky quartz*
Verena Darlath, Diplom Graduation work

2009 „Brosche 10" Brosche | *brooch*
Recon®, Zinn, Stahl | *Recon®, tin, steel*
Mun Sun Choi, Diplom Graduation work

2013 „Toquem fusta" Halsschmuck | *necklace*
versteinertes Holz, Pink Ivory, Leder, Gold | *fossilized wood, Pink Ivory, leather, gold*
Katharina Dettar, BA Graduation work

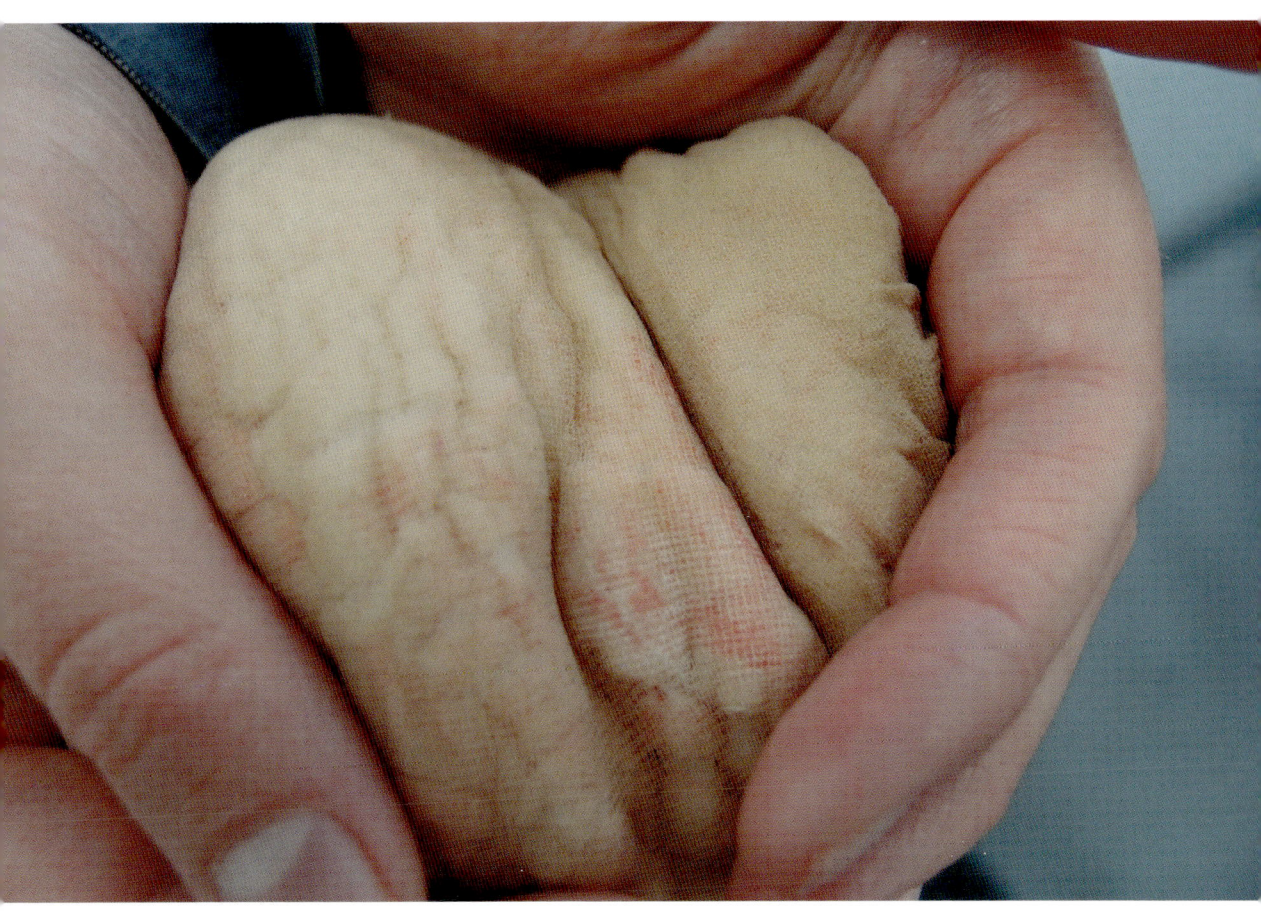

2016 Studie | *study*
Nylon, Mehl, Farbe | *nylon, flour, paint*
Stefanie Thalhammer, BFA Semester 3

2016 Schliffe | *cuts*
Bergkristall | *rock crystal*
Azhar Ali Malik, MFA Semester 2

2016 Schliffe | *cuts*
links: Rauchquarz; rechts: Bergkristall | *left: smoky quartz; right: rock crystal*
Azhar Ali Malik, MFA Semester 2

2015 „Necklace 2" Halsschmuck | *necklace*
Eisen, Basalt | *iron, basalt*
Aiza Mahmood, MFA Graduation work

2015 „Necklace 3" Halsschmuck | *necklace*
Eisen, Stein | *iron, stone*
Aiza Mahmood, MFA Graduation work

2016 „War" Halsschmuck | *necklace*
Achat, Feinsilber, Angelschnur | *agate, fine silver, fishing wire*
Yiftah Avrahamy, MFA Graduation work

2015 „Shahnaz" Halsschmuck | *necklace*
Zement, Aluminium, Gießharz, Pigment, PVC | *cement, aluminium, resin, pigment, PVC*
Saleema Sheikh, MFA Semester 3

2015 „Andenken 3" Haarschmuck | *hairpin*
Jade | *jade*
Kun Zhang, BFA Graduation work

Zum Studium
On the Study

Notizen zur künstlerischen Grundlehre
Eva-Maria Kollischan

Oft werde ich gefragt, warum Schmuckgestalter während des Studiums künstlerische Grundlehre erhalten, bzw. was das sei, „künstlerische Grundlehre". Auch im Unterricht oder bei der Vorbereitung taucht immer wieder die Frage auf: Worum geht es eigentlich? Welches ist der beste Weg, an ein so komplexes Thema, für das in einem Bachelorstudium wenig Zeit ist, heranzugehen? Daher nehme ich diesen Katalog zum Anlass, hierzu ein paar Gedanken zu notieren.

 Künstlerische Grundlehre richtet sich in der Regel an Menschen, die am Beginn eines Kunst- oder Designstudiums stehen. Man kann lesen, es handele sich dabei um eine Lehre, die ein künstlerisches Grundverständnis schaffen soll. Mit „Grundverständnis" sind Begriffe aus der Gestaltung gemeint: Verständnis für Form entwickeln, Übungen zu Farbe absolvieren, Spannung auf einer Fläche erzeugen, Material kennenlernen. Nach meinem eigenen Verständnis als Künstlerin, die in der Lehre tätig ist, geht es neben Ausprobieren und Experimentieren zunächst darum, „eine Erfahrung" zu machen. Dabei gibt es kein „richtig" oder „falsch", sondern es soll tatsächlich etwas erfahren oder erlebt werden. Und zwar in der analogen, haptischen, direkten, sinnlichen Begegnung mit Material, Farbe, Form. Gemeint ist zum Beispiel die Haltung, die ein Kind hat, wenn es ein Stück Holz zum ersten Mal bewusst berührt. Was erlebt es bei der Berührung, was macht nicht nur dieses Material, sondern gerade dieses Stück einzigartig? Es geht um beiläufige Erfahrungen von Berührung und Beobachtung, die jeder mehr oder weniger bewusst schon einmal gemacht hat.

 Die Fähigkeit, durch sinnliche und direkte Wahrnehmung eine Offenheit zu erreichen ist ein wesentliches Unterrichtsziel. Jeder Studierende soll in der Lage sein, sich diese Offenheit nicht nur im Unterricht, sondern für sein ganzes Leben zu erhalten. Es ist nicht leicht, diesen Anfängergeist dauerhaft zu erreichen, denn bis zum Erwachsenenalter wurden wir bereits durch Erziehung und Erlebnisse „weg erzogen" von Offenheit, Entdeckung und Spiel. Bleiben sie aber trotz der normativen Erziehung erhalten, dann können daraus unendliche Ideen geschöpft werden, um so zu einer sinnstiftenden Arbeit zu gelangen.

 Der für mich wesentliche Aspekt der künstlerischen Grundlehre ist ein „veränderter Blick". Der Blick, mit dem ich die Welt sehe, der Blick mit dem ich durch die Stadt gehe, mein Blick, wenn er zufällig auf eine Hausfassade fällt oder auf ein Auto oder auf ein beliebiges Objekt, das meine Aufmerksamkeit und mein Interesse zunächst nicht im Geringsten weckt. Ich kann durch die Stadt gehen mit dem Gedanken an den nächsten Termin und an meine Aufgaben. Mit Gedanken an Vergangenes, an zu Erledigendes und ich kann durch

Notes on Teaching the Basics of Art

Eva-Maria Kollischan

I am often asked why jewellery designers are taught the basics of art while they are studying or I am looked at with amazement: what's that, then, 'the basics of art'? In the classroom situation or during preparation the question also often arises of what this is all about. And above all: what is the best way of approaching a subject that is so complex and for which there is little time in a course of study leading to a bachelor's degree? Hence I am taking this catalogue as an opportunity to jot down a few thoughts on the subject.

Teaching the fundamentals of art is, as a rule, aimed at people who are beginning to study art or design. One can read this as teaching that is supposed to create a basic understanding of art. 'A basic understanding' means concepts from the field of design: developing an understanding of form, finishing classwork on colour, creating tension on a surface, becoming acquainted with material. According to my understanding as an artist who works in teaching, what is involved, along with trial and error and experimentation, is, first of all, experiencing. Nor is there any right or wrong about it. Instead something must be experienced or lived through. And in analogue, tactile, direct, sensory encounters with material, colour, form. What is meant by this is, for example, the attitude a child assumes when it has touched a piece of wood deliberately for the first time. What does that child experience in touching, what makes not just this material but this particular piece unique? This is about casual experiences of touching and observing that everyone has had at some time more or less consciously.

An important aim of classroom teaching is inculcating receptivity through sensory and direct perception. Every student should be able not only to learn this receptivity in the classroom but to retain it for his or her whole life. It isn't easy to attain this beginner's spirit on a permanent basis because by the time we have reached adulthood, openmindedness, discovery and play have already been 'taught out' of us by upbringing and experience. If these qualities have, however, been retained despite a normative upbringing, they can be a source of infinite ideas through which one can arrive at meaningful work.

The crucial aspect of teaching the basics of art is 'changing the eye'. The eye with which I see the world, the eye with which I walk through a city, my eye when it rests by chance on a house façade or a car or any object whatsoever that neither attracts my attention nor arouses my interest in the slightest at first sight. I can be walking through a city with my mind on my next deadline and my duties. With thoughts of the past, of what must be taken care of. And

die Stadt gehen und die Umwelt mit ihrer sichtbaren Oberfläche als mein Material betrachten. Ein wesentlicher Sinn von künstlerischer Erfahrung ist, diesen Blick nachhaltig offen für die Welt und ihre formalen wie inhaltlichen Erlebnisse zu machen. Wie können Menschen dazu angeregt werden – langfristig – die Welt mit offenen Augen zu sehen, als Möglichkeit und Quelle für jegliche Gestaltungsideen? Künstlerische Gestaltung dreht sich um die Frage: Welche Möglichkeiten habe ich, ein Stück Papier zu betrachten, oder ein Blatt, das vom Baum gefallen ist, oder einen Plastikbecher, den ich auf der Straße finde.

Seitdem ich mich, zunächst als Studentin – später als Dozentin, mit Grundlehre beschäftige, hat sich rund um diesen Aspekt des veränderten Blicks, der für mich den Kern der Grundlehre ausmacht, vieles verändert. Zeit für die Grundlehre, wie sie zu meiner eigenen Studienzeit gelehrt wurde, existiert nicht mehr. Es gab ein Grund- und ein Hauptstudium, welche durch eine Zwischenprüfung voneinander getrennt waren. Die Grundlehre war im Grundstudium untergebracht. Sie sollte eine breite Basis schaffen für eine Vertiefung von einzelnen Fächern im Hauptstudium. Dies wurde in Übungen zu verschiedenen Themen aufeinander aufbauend gelehrt, wie beispielsweise Zeichnung und Farbe. Danach erst wurde im dreidimensionalen Bereich gearbeitet. Als eine der Folgen der europaweiten Umstellung der Diplomstudiengänge auf Bachelor und Master ist das Grundstudium als fester Bestandteil weitgehend verschwunden. Künstlerische Grundlehre wird jetzt vom ersten Semester an parallel zu den Hauptfächern gelehrt und Lern- und vor allem Erfahrungsinhalte stehen in einem anderen, in der Regel zielorientierteren Kontext. Oft wird diese Veränderung als Verlust dargestellt und als Mangel an Basis, auf welcher aufbauend sich später eine ausgereifte Persönlichkeit als Künstler oder Gestalter entwickeln könnte.

Ich kann einzelne Kritikpunkte gut nachvollziehen, sehe diese Entwicklung insgesamt jedoch nicht als Verlust, sondern auch in der Grundlehre als Chance und Möglichkeit umzudenken. Alles befindet sich in Veränderung: wir selbst, unsere Umwelt, unsere Gesellschaft, also auch die künstlerische Grundlehre. Ich verstehe das als Herausforderung und als Ansporn, wach zu bleiben, und als Beweis, dass es nicht darum gehen kann, Wissen anzusammeln, das dann in einem Teil unseres Gehirns lagert, um von dort immer wieder abgerufen zu werden. Auch unser Wissen ist in Veränderung begriffen. Jeder von uns baut an einem Reservoir, das er im Lauf des Lebens weiter entwickelt und das sich nicht zu Ende bringen lässt, das gar kein Ende haben kann.

Dieser Prozess fordert in der Lehre ein verändertes Herangehen und einen veränderten Umgang mit den Lehrinhalten. Der klassische Aufbau mit einfachen Übungen, mit Trennung in zwei- und dreidimensionales Gestalten in verschiedenen Kursen, mit Studien zum Erfahren der Materialeigenschaften ist

I can go through a city and observe my surroundings with their visible surface as my material. An essential meaning of artistic experience is opening this eye lastingly to the world and the formal and semantic experiences it offers. How can people be inspired – over the long term – to see the world with open eyes as a possibility for, and source of, all sorts of design ideas? Designing art is about the question of what possibilities I have for observing a sheet of paper or a leaf that has fallen from a tree or an empty plastic cup I find in the street.

Ever since I have been preoccupied – at first as a student, later as an instructor – with the basics of art, much has changed around this aspect of changing one's eye, which for me constitutes the core of those fundamentals. Time for the basics of art as it was taught to me during my own student years no longer exists. There used to be a foundation course and a main course that were separated from each other by an intermediate exam. The basics of art were assigned to the foundation course. It was supposed to create a broad base for the in-depth study of individual subjects in the main course. This was taught in lessons on the various subjects that built on each other – for instance, drawing and colour. Only after that did students work in three-dimensional fields. One of the consequences of the switch throughout Europe to courses of study leading to bachelor's and master's degrees is that foundation courses as an integral part of a course of study have for the most part disappeared. The fundamentals of art are now taught from the first term on in parallel with the main subjects, and learning content and, more importantly, experience content are in a different context, as a rule in a goal-oriented one. This change is often decried as a loss and as lacking a foundation on which an artist or designer used to be able to build to develop a mature personality.

It's easy for me to understand why individual points are criticised, but still I view this development as a whole not as a loss but, even in teaching the basics, as an opportunity and possibility for rethinking. Everything is changing: we ourselves, our environment, our society, so, too, are the basics of art. I view this as a challenge and as an incentive for staying alert and as proof that amassing knowledge that is then stored in some part of our brain to be retrieved from there at need cannot be the purpose of such teaching. Our knowledge is also changing. Every one of us is building up a reservoir that we develop further over the course of our lives and that cannot be brought to an end; that cannot have an end at all.

This process calls for a change in approach and a change in dealing with teaching content. The classic structure with simple classroom teaching, with division into designing in two and three dimensions in different courses, with courses on experiencing the properties of materials, is only possible to a limit-

in einem sechssemestrigen Bachelorstudium nur noch eingeschränkt möglich. Die Lehre der Grundlagen ist daher nun viel stärker auf den Kontext bezogen, reagiert auf aktuelle Ereignisse, Aufgaben, Ausstellungen, Herausforderungen, was in einem Studium der Angewandten Kunst sehr wünschenswert ist. So erfolgt die Lehre heute in Projektarbeit, die kaum aufeinander aufbaut, sondern wie Blitzlicht einzelne Ereignisse beleuchtet. Jeder Studierende ist wesentlich stärker gefordert, seine Themen und Inhalte zu finden und von Anfang an die für ihn relevanten Techniken und Formen zu erkennen und dann zu vertiefen. Auch die Lehrenden sind entsprechend stark herausgefordert, die Lehre möglichst zu individualisieren. Die Grundlehre ist mehr Anregung durch Übung als breite Grundlagenkenntnis. Sie kann Impulse geben, und sie soll vor allem Interesse, Neugier und Offenheit erzeugen, die anhaltend sind. Dies bedeutet einen höheren Anspruch an die Fähigkeit der Studierenden, sich auf Neues und Unbekanntes, bzw. Inhalte, die nicht einzuordnen sind, einzulassen.

In der modernen Bildungspolitik erleben wir einen weitverbreiteten, gesellschaftlich bedingten Ruf nach Interdisziplinarität und es finden inhaltlich fortwährende Prozesse der Verknappung der Zeit statt. Gleichzeitig leben wir in einer Welt, die immer komplexer wird. Daher ist es heute nicht mehr sinnvoll, die Erfahrungen in der Grundlehre einzig auf die Beobachtung und Untersuchung von Skulptur im Bezug zum Körper zu richten. Dreidimensionalität, Material sowie Tragbarkeit und Körperbezug verorten Schmuck in der Skulptur. Abgesehen von diesem sehr wichtigen skulpturalen Aspekt geht es auch primär darum, die Welt „draußen" mit einzubeziehen und als Schmuckschaffende oder -schaffender eine inhaltliche Bedeutung entsprechend der gesellschaftlich notwendigen Relevanz des Schmucks erwirken zu können. Auch Schmuckgestalter leben in einer Welt der Globalisierung, in einer Welt der Veränderung Europas, in einer Welt mit Flüchtlings- und Migrantenströmen und Wirtschaftskrisen. In unserer Welt, in der sich Zentren verlagern, in der täglich von Krieg und Terror berichtet wird, kann auch Schmuck mit künstlerischem Anspruch nicht einfach nur Material am Körper bleiben. Die Bedeutung von Schmuck als Äußerung zu gesellschaftlich und persönlich relevanten Themen muss daher auch als Basis und Impuls in die Grundlehre einfließen. Die Herausforderung für die Grundlehre besteht daher heute darin, einen Spagat herzustellen zwischen direkten, sinnlichen Erlebnissen, die Material-Wahrnehmung und Material-Gesetze umfassen, und gleichzeitig die Komplexität der Welt nicht außen vor zu lassen. Dies sollte Ansporn sein, trotz Hiobsbotschaften und Unübersichtlichkeit allerorten eine Erfahrung machen zu wollen und deswegen immer wieder neu an die „alten" Themen heranzugehen, sie immer wieder „in die Hand" zu nehmen und mit aktuellem Bezug neu zu überdenken.

ed extent within a course of study leading to a bachelor's degree in six terms. Hence teaching the basics of art is now much more strongly context-oriented, reacts to current events, tasks, exhibitions, challenges, which is highly desirable in a course of study in applied art. So teaching takes place nowadays in project work, with hardly any project building on another. Instead, individual events are illumined as if by a photo flash. What is required of students to a considerably great extent now is finding their own themes and content and realising from the outset what techniques and forms are relevant for them and then go into them in depth. Teachers, too, are accordingly faced with the daunting challenge of individualising what they teach as far as possible. Teaching the basics of art is stimulation by practice rather than inculcating a broad-based knowledge of basic principles. It can provide stimuli and above all it is supposed to generate interest, curiosity and receptivity that are lasting. This means expecting more of students' capacity for letting themselves in for new and unknown things, or content that cannot be pigeon-holed.

In modern education policy we are experiencing a widespread socially conditioned call for interdisciplinarity, and processes are taking place that are leading to a shortage of time for content. At the same time we are living in a world that is growing ever more complex. Hence it no longer makes sense nowadays to aim experience solely at observing and investigating sculpture in relation to the body. Three-dimensionality and material as well as wearability and the relationship to the body place jewellery in sculpture. Apart from this very important sculptural aspect, what is primarily at stake is including the world 'outside' and, as men or women making jewellery, making content meaningful to match the socially necessary relevance of jewellery. Even jewellery designers are living in a globalised world, a world in which Europe is changing, a world into which refugees and migrants are pouring and which is beset with economic crises. In our world, in which centres are shifting, in which war and terror are reported on daily, even jewellery with a claim to being art cannot simply remain on the body as material. Hence the importance of jewellery as a statement on socially and personally relevant subjects must also be incorporated in teaching fundamentals as a basis and as a motivating force. The challenge that teaching the basics of art is facing consists nowadays in engaging in a balancing act between direct, sensory experiences that include perception of materials and the laws of materials and, at the same time, not neglecting the complexity of the world. This should, despite bad tidings and confusion on all sides, be an incentive to want to experience something and for that reason to keep on approaching 'old' subjects in a new way, to keep 'picking them up' and rethinking them with topical relevance.

Zur Philosophie der Fachrichtung
Theo Smeets

Die an vielen Orten seit Jahrzehnten geführte Auseinandersetzung, was Schmuck sei, Handwerk, Design oder Kunst, hat wesentlich zu einer Schärfung des Profils unserer Fachrichtung beigetragen. Es ist die zentrale Frage nach einer beruflichen Identität, an deren Beantwortung wir forschen. Die Aufgabenstellung des Schmucks, so wie wir sie heute interpretieren und verstehen, führt zu einer sich über eine Untersuchung der Verhältnisse zu benachbarten Bereichen definierenden Position:

- Schmuck ist kein Handwerk. Mit der handwerklichen Zentralstellung des meisterlichen Könnens besteht zwar eine Schnittmenge – der zeitgenössische Schmuck-Fokus ist ein anderer.
- Schmuck ist kein Design. Mit der Zentralstellung einer modischen Ästhetisierung und deren erfolgreicher Vermarktung besteht zwar eine Schnittmenge – der zeitgenössische Schmuck-Fokus ist ein anderer.
- Schmuck ist keine Freie Kunst. Mit der künstlerischen Zentralstellung des „aus sich heraus existieren" besteht zwar eine Schnittmenge – der zeitgenössische Schmuck-Fokus ist ein anderer.

Ziel dieser Positionierung ist es allerdings nicht, Abgrenzungslinien zu ziehen oder bestehende zu stärken. Die Frage nach der Identität Schmuckschaffender soll jedoch nicht nur im Rahmen bereits bestehender – aber für uns nicht hinreichender – Kriterienkataloge anderer Fachgebiete überdacht werden.

Schmuck ist Angewandte Kunst

Die Ausbildung der Studierenden geschieht elementar auf einer künstlerischen Basis – hinführend zu deren gesellschaftlicher Aufgabe hinsichtlich Schmuck und Schmücken. Edelstein und Schmuck brauchen zusätzlich und gleichzeitig zur künstlerischen Basis die Fähigkeiten des Handwerks im perfektionistischen Sinn sowie Elemente des Designs für eine zweckmäßige Ästhetik und eine taugliche Vermarktungsstrategie.

Verwunderlich ist die aktuell wahrnehmbare Vernachlässigung der Aufgabenstellung des Schmucks in der Gesellschaft. Denn das, was Schmuck eigentlich auslösen soll, ist schon sehr lange außerordentlich deutlich. Hierzu ist ein kurzer historischer Exkurs hilfreich. Schmuck ist nachgewiesenermaßen die älteste künstlerische Äußerung des Menschen hinsichtlich seines sozialen Bewusstseins: bereits auf den frühesten Höhlenmalereien sind Andeutungen an Körpern zu finden, die Schmuckstücke als identitätsstiftende Distinktion in der Gruppe, aber auch deren semantischen Gegenpart – als Gruppen-/Stammeszugehörigkeit

On Department Philosophy
Theo Smeets

The discussion that has been ongoing for decades on what jewellery is – crafts, design or art – has contributed substantially to honing the profile of our department. Answering the pivotal question of professional identity is what we are researching. The scope of jewellery as we interpret it nowadays and understand it has led via a study of its relationships with neighbouring fields to a defining position:

- Jewellery is not crafts. There is an overlap, admittedly, with the central status of consummate skill in workmanship – nonetheless, the focus of contemporary jewellery is different.
- Jewellery is not design. There is an overlap, definitely, with the central status of fashionable aestheticisation and the successful marketing of it – the focus of contemporary jewellery is nonetheless different.
- Jewellery is not fine art. There is an overlap with the central aesthetic status of 'existing for its own sake' – the focus of contemporary jewellery is different.

The aim of this positioning is certainly not to draw demarcation lines or to consolidate extant ones. The question of jewellery makers' identity is not, however, to be reconsidered solely in the context of existing catalogues of criteria taken over from other fields that are insufficient for us.

Jewellery is applied art

Students' training and education take place fundamentally on an artistic basis – leading to their social mission in respect of jewellery and personal adornment. In addition to, and synchronously with, the artistic basis, gemstones and jewellery need the capabilities of crafts in the perfectionist sense as well as elements of design for an appropriate aesthetic and a viable marketing strategy.

What is surprising is the currently perceptible neglect of the mission jewellery can and should have in society. After all, what jewellery is actually expected to spark off has been extraordinarily obvious for a very long time. A brief historical digression is helpful on this. Jewellery is verifiably man's earliest artistic expression respecting his social awareness: hints of it already occur on bodies in the earliest cave paintings that document pieces of jewellery as an identity-establishing distinction in the group as well as its semantic counterpart – as an indicator of group/tribal membership. At this point, with the aid of a temporal and cultural change in perspective, the role played by the adorned persons is to be considered, the knowledge they possessed that put them in the position of

zuweisend – dokumentieren. An der Stelle angelangt, sollte mithilfe zeitlicher und kultureller Perspektivwechsel in Betracht gezogen werden, welche Rolle die geschmückten Personen innehatten, welches Wissen sie in sich vereinten, damit sie in der Lage waren, die Objekte, Totems, Amulette etc. mit Bedeutung aufzuladen. Diese, immer mit einer gesellschaftlichen (Aus)Wirkung verbundene Aufgabe macht Schmuck unverkennbar zu Angewandter Kunst.

Für uns als Hochschule ergibt sich die anschließende zentrale Frage für die Gestaltung der Studiengänge Edelstein und Schmuck: Wie können wir mithilfe der gewonnenen soziologischen Erkenntnisse, die für unser Berufsprofil notwendigen sozial-empathischen Kompetenzen im Studium generieren, aktivieren und stimulieren?

Aufgabe und Verantwortung

In der modernen Gesellschaft wird die Auseinandersetzung mit der Erschaffung personaler Bedeutungsträger weitgehend Handwerk und Design überlassen. Schmuck wird folglich unter einem unvollständigen Kriteriensatz geschaffen, betrachtet und bewertet.

Als personaler Gegenstand benötigt Schmuck unbestreitbar eine distinktive oder aber verbindende Bedeutungsebene, die sich auch in den Konsumentenbedürfnissen und -erwartungen widerspiegelt. Die Fachrichtung knüpft an solche Bedeutungsebenen aktiv an und stellt in den Studiengängen neben die bildnerisch-künstlerische eine profunde Auseinandersetzung mit gesellschaftlichen, (inter)kulturellen, ethno- und soziologischen sowie historischen Fragestellungen.

Die Feststellung der Schnittmengen mit Kunst, Handwerk und Design, die Fragestellung nach dem Sinn des Schmucks bzw. nach der sozialen Aufgabe solcher personaler Gegenstände und die sich daraus ergebende Suche nach der gesellschaftlichen Verantwortung der Schmuckschaffenden bilden zusammen ein Wissens- und Bewusstseinspotenzial. So ist es naheliegend, für die Suche nach Antworten, Lösungen und Ergebnissen zunächst einen eigenen (Frei)Raum erneut in Anspruch zu nehmen: Angewandte Kunst. Das mittels eines solchen Freiraums kreierte Selbstverständnis des eigenen Terrains bietet sodann klarere Perspektiven, die vorhin formulierte Aufgabenstellung in der modernen Gesellschaft zu aktualisieren und sinnvoll zu erfüllen. Die Fachrichtung befindet sich stets mitten in dieser Diskussion.

Angewandte Kunst in der Lehre

„Das Wesen der Lehre findet sich in dem lateinischen Wort *professio*: Stellungnahme, Erklärung. Für Professorinnen und Professoren bedeutet das, eine Erklä-

loading those objects, totems, amulets and so on with meaning. This task, always associated with its social impact, makes jewellery unmistakeably applied art.

For us as a university of applied sciences, the pivotal question related to designing the gemstone and jewellery courses is as follows: how can we with the aid of sociological knowledge that has been gained generate, activate and stimulate in the course of study the socio-empathic competences that are necessary for our professional profile?

Mission and responsibility

In modern society the investigation of the creation of personal semantic vehicles is largely left up to crafts and design. Consequently, jewellery is created, observed and evaluated according to an incomplete set of criteria.

As a personal object, jewellery undisputedly needs a distinctive or associational semantic plane that is also reflected in consumer needs and expectations. The department actively links up with such semantic planes and offers in the courses, apart from the visual and artistic side, a profound investigation of social, (inter)cultural, ethnological and sociological as well as historical issues.

Confirmation that art, crafts and design overlap, the question of the meaning of jewellery or the social mission of such personal objects, and jewellery makers' quest for social responsibility resulting from it together form a potential for knowledge and awareness. Hence it would seem obvious to again lay claim to a specific (free) space in the search for answers, solutions and results: applied art. Awareness of having created a territory of its own by means of a free space of this kind then provides clearer perspectives on actualising the previously defined jewellery maker's mission in modern society and fulfilling it meaningfully. The department is invariably involved in this discussion.

Applied art in teaching

'The quintessence of teaching is contained in the Latin word *professio*: declaration, profession, explanation. For the men and women who are professors that means making a statement about their own convictions that is not always easy for students to accept under all circumstances. Teaching in the field of art does not aim at the pleasure or sovereignty of students as consumers of knowledge.'[1] The attitude to studying thus called for leads as an operative concept to the strategic meta-aim of the critical woman or critical man as an artist: seemingly

---

1   'The consumer model implies that the university provides "services". Seminars and courses are developed according to the needs of students, who view themselves as consumers, who pick up their degrees comfortably and without much effort just like shopping.' Trebor Scholz, *New-Media Art Education and Its Discontents*, Art Journal of the College Art Association of America, vol. 64, no. 1 (Spring 2005), pp. 95–108.

rung der eigenen Überzeugungen abzugeben, die für Studierende nicht unter allen Umständen leicht zu akzeptieren ist. Lehre im künstlerischen Bereich zielt nicht auf Wohlgefallen oder auf die Souveränität von Studierenden als Konsumierende von Wissen."[1] Diese geforderte Studierhaltung führt als operatives Konzept zum strategischen Meta-Ziel der kritischen Künstlerin bzw. des kritischen Künstlers: scheinbar gegensätzliche Phänomene – die des einerseits autark-egozentrischen und andererseits des sozial-empathischen Kunstschaffenden – gilt es zu vereinen.

Der Campus Idar-Oberstein ist solch ein Ort der Auseinandersetzung im Spannungsfeld zwischen künstlerischer Bildung einerseits und wissenschaftlicher Lehre und Forschung andererseits. Mit dem Studienangebot besetzt die Fachrichtung ein Feld der Angewandten Kunst und stellt sich ihren Aufgaben- und Fragenstellungen bezüglich des Schmückens auf einer formal-künstlerischen und inhaltlich-gesellschaftlichen Ebene. So werden Absolventinnen und Absolventen in die Lage versetzt, aktiv nachhaltige Handlungsszenarien für die Auseinandersetzung mit zeitgenössischen personalen Symbolen in Form „tragbarer Objekte" zu entwickeln.

Das Studienprogramm orientiert sich an Qualifikationszielen, die fachliche und überfachliche Aspekte in den Bereichen von künstlerischer Eignung, Befähigung zum zivilgesellschaftlichen Engagement und Persönlichkeitsentwicklung umfassen. Neben der fachlichen Förderung wird auch die künstlerische Kompetenz, Kommunikationsvermögen, Methodenorientierung, Koordinations-, Organisations- und Moderationskompetenz hinsichtlich der künstlerischen Betätigung vorangetrieben.

Identität: zur künstlerischen Verantwortung in der Gesellschaft

Die künstlerische Identität der Schmuckschaffenden kann wie wir festgestellt haben also nicht als „irgendwo in der Mitte zwischen autonomer Kunst, Design und Handwerk" definiert werden.

Mittels einer erweiterten Befähigung sollten Absolventinnen und Absolventen in die Lage versetzt worden sein, auf die unterschiedlichen Rollen der Trägerinnen und Träger, der Betrachterinnen und Betrachter sowie die der Schmuckschaffenden fokussieren zu können. Es besteht Konsens, dass Kunst Fragen stellen muss in einer bestimmten notwendigen Abstraktion. Design dagegen liefert im Idealfall brauchbare und funktionierende, ästhetisch anspre-

---

[1] „Das Konsumierenden-Modell unterstellt, dass die Hochschule ‚Dienstleistungen' anbietet. Seminare und Kurse werden nach den Bedürfnissen von Studierenden entwickelt, die sich selbst als Konsumierende verstehen, die sich ganz bequem und ohne große Anstrengung eben wie beim Shopping ihren Abschluss holen." T. Scholz: *New-Media Art Education and Its Discontents*, in: Art Journal of the College Art Association of America, H. 64, 1/2005, S. 95–108.

contradictory phenomena – on the one hand, the autarchy of the egocentric and, on the other, the socio-empathic creator of art – must be united in one.

The Idar-Oberstein campus is a place of this kind for discussion in the charged field between training artists on the one hand and, on the other, academic teaching and research. With the curriculum it offers, the department occupies an applied-arts field and has assigned itself tasks and questions related to adornment on the formal, artistic and semantic-social planes. Thus graduates are enabled to develop sustainable scenarios for active behaviour in the discussion with contemporary personal symbols in the form of 'wearable objects'.

The programme of studies is aligned with qualification targets that include both subject-specific and interdisciplinary aspects in the areas of artistic aptitude, commitment to engaging competently in civil society, and personality development. Alongside promoting subject-related skills and knowledge, the programme ensures that both hard and soft skills such as artistic competence, communication skills, a focus on methodology, and skills in coordination, organisation and presentation with respect to working in art are furthered.

Identity: on artistic responsibility in society

Hence, as we have ascertained, the artistic identity of jewellery designers and makers cannot be defined as 'somewhere on the continuum between autonomous art, design and crafts'.

By means of capability enlargement, graduates are to be put in the position of being able to focus on the varying roles of men and women as wearers of jewellery, men and women as observers of jewellery and those of the jewellery designer and maker. There is agreement on the fact that art must ask questions in a particular necessary abstraction. Design, on the other hand, provides, in the ideal case, useful and functional tools that are aesthetically attractive and often enjoyable. Jewellery possesses the unique distinction of creating an intrinsic link between our origins (that is, social, ethnic, geographic, emotional and so on) and our surroundings at a given time. Thus possibilities emerge for perceiving changes in our immediate environment, documenting them in identity-establishing objects and reacting adequately.

To reach the point that an artwork can trigger off those processes, planes must be incorporated in a work other than merely those that address the questions of form, colour, material, production and marketing. Here students are challenged to link their sensory experiences with their thinking and acting within society in a way that is both active and sustainable.

To meet the requirements of a socio-empathic identity enlarged in the above sense commensurately in a work, jewellery should contain ethical and

chende und oftmals vergnügliche Werkzeuge. Schmuck besitzt die einzigartige Eigenart, eine intrinsische Verbindung zwischen unserer Herkunft (also: sozial, ethnisch, geografisch, emotional, etc.) und unserer momentanen Umgebung herzustellen. So entstehen Möglichkeiten, Veränderungen in unserem Umfeld wahrzunehmen, sie in identitätsstiftenden Gegenständen zu dokumentieren und adäquat zu reagieren.

Um dahin zu gelangen, dass ein Kunstwerk diese Prozesse auslösen kann, sind andere Ebenen in der Arbeit einzubeziehen als lediglich solche, die Fragen zur Form, Farbe, Material, Produktion und Marketing stellen. Hier sind die Studierenden aufgefordert, aktiv und nachhaltig ihre sinnlichen Erfahrungen mit ihrem Denken und Handeln innerhalb der Gesellschaft zu verknüpfen.

Um den Anforderungen einer dahingehend erweiterten sozio-empathischen Identität in der Arbeit angemessen zu begegnen, soll Schmuck über die ästhetische Position hinaus zumindest ethisch-philosophische Aspekte enthalten, die unser Zusammenleben reflektieren. Dafür ist auf einer Meta-Ebene ein impliziter Diskurs zwischen der sozialen Positionierung der jeweiligen Arbeit hinsichtlich Symbolik, Semantik und nicht zuletzt der eigenen Ikonographie vonnöten. Wenn dieser Diskurs stattfindet, dann steht der Kunstschaffende sozusagen unter der impliziten (Selbst-)Verpflichtung, das eigene Schaffen und die eigenen künstlerischen Strategien zu hinterfragen, zu evaluieren und zu überarbeiten, damit auch künftig gesellschaftliche Bedeutung innerhalb eines zeitgenössischen Kontexts vorhanden sein kann.

Als Grundlage für den Schaffensprozess bedeutet das eine schier endlose Zirkelbewegung: Kunstschaffende reflektieren die sie umgebenden Prozesse und Empfindlichkeiten, indem sie ein Stück kreieren. Die Arbeit erringt einen Platz innerhalb der Gesellschaft und verändert diese. Die Umwelt reagiert, die Kunstschaffenden registrieren die Reaktion und setzen ihre Erfahrung in weitere Stücke um. Der künstlerische Input ist in diesem „Perpetuum Mobile" die Energie, die den Kreislauf antreibt. Das Ergebnis ist ein permanentes Update der Gegenstände, eine unaufhörliche Veränderung, die Teil der geistigen Evolution ist. Auf diese Weise bleibt Kunst – hier: Schmuck – in Verbindung mit der Gesellschaft. Und zwar nicht vorrangig gelenkt von Marketingstrategien, merkantilen Werten oder modischer Kurzlebigkeit. Wenn sie frei von schnelllebiger ästhetischer Abstumpfung ist, kann diese Herangehensweise Modelle mit der impliziten Absicht liefern, die fortwährende mentale, emotionale und/oder soziale Entwicklung relativ kurzfristig erfassbar zu machen. Die Arbeiten bekommen eine identitätsstiftende Potenz.

philosophical aspects that reflect our communal lives above and beyond the aesthetic stance it represents. For this to come about, an implicit discourse on a meta-level is needed between the social positioning of a given work with respect to symbolism, semantics and, not least, its creator's own iconography. When this discourse takes place, the person creating art is confronted, so to speak, with the implicit (self-imposed) obligation to question the assumptions of his or her work and artistic strategies, to evaluate and rework them so that even in the future social significance can be present within a contemporary context.

As the basis for the creative process, that means a sheer endless hermeneutic circle: artists reflect the processes and sensibilities surrounding them by making a piece. The work attains a status within society and changes that society. The environment reacts; the artists register the reaction and translate their experience into more pieces. The artistic input in this 'perpetuum mobile' is the energy that drives the cycle. The result is a permanent updating of the objects, a ceaseless change that is part of intellectual and spiritual evolution. In this way art – here: jewellery – remains connected to society. And indeed not primarily steered by marketing strategies, mercantile values or the ephemerality of fashion. If it is free of the aesthetically stupefying quality of being fast-paced, this approach can provide models with the implicit intention of making continual mental, emotional and/or social development understandable on relatively short notice. The works gain identity-establishing potential.

Autorenbiografien | Authors' Biographies

Ute Eitzenhöfer, Dipl.-Des. (*1969)

studierte nach Abschluss der Goldschmiedelehre an der Hochschule Pforzheim im Studiengang Schmuck und Gerät (1992–1996). Seit 1996 ist sie freiberuflich als Schmuckgestalterin sowohl im künstlerischen als auch im seriellen Bereich tätig. Ihre Vita weist zahlreiche nationale und internationale Ausstellungen und Ausstellungsbeteiligungen aus und sie ist mit ihren Arbeiten in öffentlichen und privaten Sammlungen vertreten. Seit 2005 ist sie Professorin für Edelstein- und Objektgestaltung an der Hochschule Trier, Fachrichtung Edelstein und Schmuck in Idar-Oberstein.

studied at the Pforzheim University of Applied Sciences (1992–1996), Department for Jewellery and Tableware, after completing a goldsmith's apprenticeship. Since 1996 she has been working as a freelance jewellery designer both in the artistic and serial fields. She has exhibited many times nationally and internationally and her work is represented in both public and private collections. Since 2005 she has held the position of Professor of Gemstone and Object Design at the Trier University of Applied Sciences, Department of Gemstones and Jewellery, in Idar-Oberstein.

Eva-Maria Kollischan (*1966)

studierte freie Kunst an den Kunstakademien Münster und München und Kommunikationsdesign an der Technischen Hochschule Nürnberg Georg Simon Ohm. Seit 2000 ist sie als freischaffende Künstlerin tätig, mit Ausstellungen und Ausstellungsbeteiligungen im In- und Ausland. Seit 2014 ist sie Professorin für künstlerische Gestaltung an der Hochschule Trier, Fachrichtung Edelstein und Schmuck in Idar-Oberstein.

studied fine art at the Academies of Fine Arts in Munster and Munich and communication design at the Georg Simon Ohm University of Applied Sciences Nuremberg. Since 2000 she has been working as a freelance artist with solo and group exhibitions both at home and abroad. Since 2014 she has held the position of Professor for Artistic Design at the Trier University of Applied Sciences, Department of Gemstones and Jewellery, in Idar-Oberstein.

Wilhelm Lindemann (*1949)

ist freiberuflicher Kurator und Autor. Langjährige Tätigkeit als Kurator, Festival- und Kulturmanager. Als Theaterproduzent Zusammenarbeit u.a. mit Teatret Cantabile 2 (DK), The Living Theatre (US), Donald Byrd Dance Company (US), Tanzcompagnie Rubato (DE) und Hanna Schygulla (FR). Seit 2001 Projektleiter der Restaurierung des Industriedenkmals Historische Uhrketten- und Bijouteriefabrik Bengel in Idar-Oberstein und dessen Ausbau zum Kulturdenkmal. Seit 2005 Kurator des wissenschaftlichen Colloquiums SchmuckDenken an der Hochschule Trier, Campus Idar-Oberstein und diverser Schmuckausstellungen.

is a freelance curator and writer. He has worked for many years as a curator and manager of festivals and cultural events. As a theatre producer he has collaborated with Teatret Cantabile 2 (DK), The Living Theatre (US), the Donald Byrd Dance Company (US), Tanzcompagnie Rubato (DE) and Hanna Schygulla (FR). Since 2001 he has headed the project for restoring and converting to a cultural monument the Historic Bengel Watchchain and Bijouterie Factory, a historic industrial building in Idar-Oberstein. Since 2005 he has curated ThinkingJewellery, an academic colloquium at the Trier University of Applied Sciences, Idar-Oberstein campus, and a wide range of jewellery exhibitions.

Theo Smeets (*1964)

lernte Gold- und Silberschmieden an der Vakschool Schoonhoven und studierte anschließend an der Gerrit Rietveld Academie in Amsterdam Schmuckgestaltung bei Onno Boekhoudt und Marjan Unger (1986–1992). Er ist seit 1992 selbstständig tätig und hat in Europa, den USA und Japan ausgestellt. 1994 Umzug von Amsterdam nach Berlin, 1998 wurde er zum Professor für Schmuck- und Objektgestaltung an der Hochschule Trier, Fachrichtung Edelstein und Schmuck in Idar-Oberstein berufen.

learnt gold- and silversmithing at the Vakschool Schoonhoven and subsequently studied jewellery design at the Gerrit Rietveld Academy in Amsterdam under Onno Boekhoudt and Marjan Unger (1986–1992). Since 1992 he has been freelance and has exhibited in Europe, the USA and Japan. He moved from Amsterdam to Berlin in 1994 and in 1998 was appointed Professor of Jewellery and Object Design at the Trier University of Applied Sciences, Department of Gemstones and Jewellery, in Idar-Oberstein.

Dr. Marjan Unger (*1946)

studierte industrielle Gestaltung an der Kunstnijverheidsschool – Hochschule für Angewandte Kunst Amsterdam (1964–1967). Studium der Kunstgeschichte an der Universität von Amsterdam. Studienschwerpunkte: Zeitgenössische Kunst, Mode und Textilgestaltung, Architektur, industrielle Archäologie und Kunstgeschichte von China und Japan (1974–1987). Dozentinnentätigkeit an der Gerrit Rietveld Academie, Amsterdam (1982–2006). Leiterin des Studiengangs Freie Gestaltung am Sandberg Institut – postgraduale Ausbildung an der Gerrit Rietveld Academie, Amsterdam (1995–2006). Chefredakteurin von Morf, Zeitschrift für Gestaltung für Studierende (2004–2008). Promotion an der Universität Leiden (2009). Zahlreiche Publikationen und Vorträge mit dem Schwerpunkt zeitgenössischer Schmuck und Mode. Vielfache Organisation von Symposien und Ausstellungen. Umfangreiche Jury-, Kommissions- und Beratungstätigkeit.

studied industrial design at the Kunstnijverheidsschool – Amsterdam Art Institute (1964–1967) and art history at Amsterdam University. Her fields of specialisation are contemporary art, fashion and textile design, architecture, industrial archaeology and Chinese and Japanese art history (1974–1987). She was a lecturer at the Gerrit Rietveld Academy in Amsterdam (1982–2006) and head of the Free Design course at the Sandberg Institute – postgraduate studies at the Gerrit Rietveld Academy in Amsterdam (1995–2006). Furthermore, she was the editor of Morf, a design magazine for students (2004–2008) and received her doctorate at Leiden University (2009). She has published numerous publications and lectures focusing on contemporary jewellery and fashion and has organised a wide range of symposia and exhibitions as well as frequently sitting on art juries and committees and engaging in art consultancy work.

Julia Wild, M.A. (*1970)

ist seit 2010 wissenschaftliche Mitarbeiterin der Fachrichtung Edelstein und Schmuck an der Hochschule Trier. Sie studierte Germanistik und Geschichte an der Ruprecht-Karls-Universität Heidelberg. Ihre Schwerpunkte liegen auf den Themen Ritual und symbolische Kommunikation, Raum und Körper, die sie in der Lehre mit dem sozialen Phänomen Schmuck in Verbindung zu bringen sucht.

has been an academic assistant at the Department of Gemstones and Jewellery at the Trier University of Applied Sciences since 2010. She studied German studies and history at the Heidelberg University. Her focus lies in the field of ritual and symbolic communication, space and body, which she seeks to bring together in her teaching with the social phenomenon of jewellery.

Team | Staff

Folgende Personen haben die in diesem Katalog vorgestellten Studierenden und Alumni ausgebildet und begleitet | the following staff have educated and supported the students and graduates presented in this catalogue:

ProfessorInnen | Professors
Edelstein | Gemstone
Ute Eitzenhöfer (seit | since 2005)
Schmuck | Jewellery
Theo Smeets (seit | since 1998)
Künstlerische Grundlagen | Basics of Art
Eva-Maria Kollischan (seit | since 2014)
Lothar Brügel (1994 – 2013)

Wissenschaftliche MitarbeiterInnen | Educational Staff
Edelstein und Schmuck | Gemstones and Jewellery
Jutta Kallfelz (seit | since 2013)
Tabea Reulecke (2007 – 2013)
Sally Kiss (2005 – 2007)
Fotografie | Photography
Cornelia Wruck (seit | since 2011)
Hartmut Becker (1991 – 2010)
Marketing | Marketing
Katharina Reimann (2015 – 2016)
Valeska Link (2009 – 2014)
Theorie | Theory
Julia Wild (seit | since 2010)

MitarbeiterInnen | Staff
Edelsteinschleife | Gemstone Workshop
Winfried Juchem (seit | since 1989)
Bibliothek | Library
Oranna Kammann (seit | since 2000)
Computer- und Studienservice | Computer and Student Service
Heinz Hub (seit | since 1993)
Sekretariat | Secretariate
Ute Schoppet (seit | since 2016)
Renate Kley (2000 – 2016)
Hausmeister | Concierge
Wolfgang Rogoll (seit | since 2012)
Werner Herrmann (1989 – 2012)
Reinigungspersonal | Cleaning Staff
Brigitte Mohn (seit | since 2000)
Gabriele Gerster (seit | since 2013)
Lisa Hertrich (1992 – 2012)

Register | Index

Aghaei, Sharareh (IR) 260/261
Almeida Meza, Adriana (CO) 192
Ameling, Anna (DE) 202
Arabova, Penka (BG) 236/237
Avrahamy, Yiftah (IL) 324/325
Bahmani Nik, Vesal (IR) 108
Baudler, Julia (DE) 163, 201
Bauzá, Francisca (DE) 226/227, 297
Bloemers, Anneke (NL) 135
Bocola, Julia (DE) 158/159
Boonyapan, Pornruedee (TH) 124/125
Brenes, Catalina (CR) 312/313
Britchford, Katie Jayne (AU) 296
Burton, Eva (AR) 309
Cavaller, Ignasi (ES) 266/267
Choi, Mun Sun (KR) 315
Cohn, Gabriela (AR) 254
Conrad, Sabine (DE) 235
Cremer, Charlie (DE) 78/79
Darlath, Verena (DE) 314
Denter, Carolin (DE) 153, 244/245
Dettar, Katharina (ES/DE) 316
Dluzniak, Dagmar (DE) 300
Domingues, Patrícia (PT) 268–271
Dreher, Mirjam (DE) 277
Dvorak, Petr (CZ) 187
Dyer, Matthias (DE) 106/107, 134
Dzuráková, Barbora (SK) 286
Ebert, Denise (DE) 80–85, 282
Emrich, Sina (DE) 142
Erlacher, Christina (AT) 262/263
Estrada, Nicolas (CO) 111
Faulkner, William Rudolph (US) 216, 298
Ferretti, Marcella (DE) 251
Flexer, Sabine (DE) 302
Friederich, Kim (DE) 166, 276
Friedrich, Alexander (DE) 169–171
Fuchsberger, Nina (DE) 126/127, 152, 160, 168, 225
Giorgadse, Tatjana (GE) 211–215
Golombosi, Elvira (SK) 273
Goltsios, Lina (GR) 193, 194
Gorbunova, Elena (RU) 164/165
Groh, Pia (AT) 252, 283–285
Grosch, Frauke (DE) 303

Hauser, Carmen (DE) 114–116
Higaki, Sachiyo (JP) 156/157, 184
Iglesias Barón, Ferràn (ES) 253, 320
In, Taehee (KR) 278/279
Jacobs, Anna (DE) 188/189
Jäger, SunHi (DE) 242
Jishkariani, Levan (GE) 180/181
Jones, Erika (GB) 146–151
Karg, Rebekka (DE) 120–123, 174
Kaube, Susanne (DE) 250
Kim, Hye-Shil (KR) 128/129, 186, 287, 306
Kim, Sun-Kyoung (KR) 182/183
Köditz, Katja (DE) 218–224, 307
Kong, Saerom (KR) 198/199
Kraus, Ulrike (DE) 255
Kröber, Lisa (DE) 301
Lahtinen, Salla (FI) 272
Larionova, Anastasiya (DE) 117
Lasso, Héctor (CO) 256
Le Monnier, Typhaine (FR) 176–179
Li, Tianqi (CN) 76/77, 88/89, 326
Maddox, John (DE/US) 92/93, 206/207, 310
Mahmood, Aiza (PA) 322/323
Malev, Daniela (DE) 246/247
Malik, Azhar Ali (PA) 318/319
Martí Mató, Cristina (ES) 204/205
Mihalus, Karina (DE) 264
Morawetz, Stephanie (AT) 136/137
Moreno Frías, Javier (ES) 154/155
Müller, Gina-Nadine (DE) 90/91, 234, 304/305
Münsch, Kathrin (DE) 308
Obermaier, Julia (DE) 196/197
Ou, Jiun-You (TW) 243
Pibernat, Sonia (ES) 143
Räthel, Sari (DE) 208–210
Rehermann, Silke (DE) 228/229
Reimann, Katharina (DE) 257–259
Reulecke, Tabea (DE) 230–233
Röhrig, Eva (DE) 311
Rudolph, Deborah (DE) 238/239
Saez Vilanova, Estela (ES) 217
Salim Raza, Mavash (PA) 132/133
Schmalenbach, Nils (DE) 248
Schröder, Maximilian (DE) 94–97, 161, 162, 294/295

Schwaag, Danni (DE) 240/241
Seachuga, Dana (IL) 289
Seilern-Aspang, Franziska (AT) 109, 110
Sheikh, Saleema (PA) 327
Solar, Alejandra (MX) 280/281
Sommerlad, Pia (DE) 200
Spitz, Amelie (DE) 191
Stolz, Antje (DE) 265
Storck, Anna (DE) 74/75
Tarín, Edu (ES) 130/131, 144/145
Thalhammer, Stefanie (DE) 98/99, 317
Van Oost, Nelly (FR) 185
Vanselow, Katharina (DE) 203
Wagner, Valérie (FR) 102/103
Wang, Qi (CN) 290/291, 293
Wassenberg, Rinke (NL) 100/101, 195, 288
Wehr, Sabine (DE) 140/141
Wiedau, Anne (DE) 274/275
Yuan, Tala (CN) 112/113, 138/139
Zhang, Kun (CN) 328
Zöller, Vanessa (DE) 86/87, 118, 190, 292

Impressum | Imprint

Die vorliegende Publikation erscheint anlässlich der Ausstellung Neuer Schmuck aus Idar-Oberstein im Stadtmuseum Simeonstift Trier, 27.11.2016–26.2.2017.
The present publication is published on the occasion of the exhibition New Jewellery from Idar-Oberstein at Stadtmuseum Simeonstift Trier, November 27, 2016 – February 26, 2017.

Herausgeber | Editor
Hochschule Trier, Campus Idar-Oberstein

AutorInnen | Authors
Prof. Ute Eitzenhöfer
Prof. Eva-Maria Kollischan
Wilhelm Lindemann
Prof. Theo Smeets
Dr. Marjan Unger
Julia Wild, M.A.

Projektkoordination arnoldsche
Project Coordination arnoldsche
Matthias Becher

Übersetzung | Translation
Deutsch-Englisch | German-English:
Allison Moseley, Houston, TX
Andrea Holme, Idar-Oberstein
Englisch-Deutsch | English-German:
Dr. Kurt Rehkopf, Hamburg
Niederländisch-Englisch | Dutch-English:
Ton Brouwers, Amsterdam

Korrektorat an der Hochschule
Proofreading at the University
Oranna Kammann

Grafische Gestaltung | Graphic Design
Cornelia Wruck, Eva-Maria Kollischan

Schrift | Fonts
Swift, Vesta (von | by Gerard Unger)

Offset Reproduktion | Offset Reproductions
Schwabenrepro, Stuttgart

Druck | Printed by
Gorenjski tisk, Kranj

Bibliografische Information der Deutschen Nationalbibliothek: Die Deutsche Nationalbibliothek verzeichnet diese Publikation in der Deutschen Nationalbibliografie; detaillierte bibliografische Daten sind im Internet über www.dnb.de abrufbar.
Bibliographic information published by the Deutsche Nationalbibliothek: The Deutsche Nationalbibliothek lists this publication in the Deutsche Nationalbibliografie; detailed bibliographic data are available on the Internet at www.dnb.de.

© 2016 arnoldsche Art Publishers, Stuttgart; Hochschule Trier, Campus Idar-Oberstein und die Autoren | and the authors

Alle Rechte vorbehalten. Vervielfältigung und Wiedergabe auf jegliche Weise (grafisch, elektronisch und fotomechanisch sowie der Gebrauch von Systemen zur Datenrückgewinnung) – auch in Auszügen – nur mit schriftlicher Genehmigung der arnoldsche Art Publishers, Olgastraße 137, D–70180 Stuttgart.
www.arnoldsche.com
All rights reserved. No part of this work may be reproduced or used in any form or by any means (graphic, electronic or mechanical, including photocopying or information storage and retrieval systems) without written permission from the copyright holder arnoldsche Art Publishers, Olgastraße 137, D–70180 Stuttgart.
www.arnoldsche.com

ISBN 978-3-89790-473-6

Made in Europe, 2016

Unser herzlicher Dank gilt allen, die uns in den letzten zehn Jahren unterstützt haben bei der Entwicklung der Fachrichtung Edelstein und Schmuck am Standort Idar-Oberstein, insbesondere Wilhelm Lindemann und Prof. Dr. Jörg Wallmeier.

Our heartfelt thanks go to all those who have supported us over the last ten years in developing the Department of Gemstones and Jewellery at the Idar-Oberstein campus, in particular Wilhelm Lindemann and Prof. Dr Jörg Wallmeier.

Dieses Buch entstand mit großzügiger Förderung von:
This book has been produced with the generous support of:

Bildnachweis | Photo Credits
Alle Fotorechte liegen bei den jeweiligen Studierenden und Alumni, mit Ausnahme von Seite:
All photo credits by the students and graduates except page:
172, 173 Hartmut Becker; 130, 138, 139, 160, 163, 176, 177, 225, 272, 308 Lothar Brügel; 85, 109, 110 Carolin Denter; 114–116 Karin Drochner; 89, 133, 327 Denise Ebert und Gina-Nadine Müller; 264 Ariana Kanonenberg; 93 Gerhard Kind; 153, 288, 326 Eva-Maria Kollischan; 103, 108, 191, 193, 284, 285, 302, 310, 318, 319 Michael Müller; 24, 125, 179, 187, 209, 210, 253, 266, 267, 281, 316 Manuel Ocaña; 230, 231 Thaddeus Robertson; 251 Markus Schmidt; 254, 283, 312, 324 Qi Wang; 91, 132, 190, 194, 217, 262, 313 Cornelia Wruck; 98 Anne Wiedau
© Stadtmuseum Simeonstift Trier: 77, 78, 86, 97 Benno Lutz; 74 Thomas Riehle; 81, 82, 85, 86, 89, 90, 93, 101, 102 Matthias Schmitt (Studio 54)
© VG Bild-Kunst, Bonn 2016: 93 Willi Sitte

Umschlagabbildung | Cover Illustration
Erika Jones (Hochschul- und Buchhandelsausgabe | *university and bookstore edition*)
Maximilian Schröder (Museumsausgabe | *museum edition*)

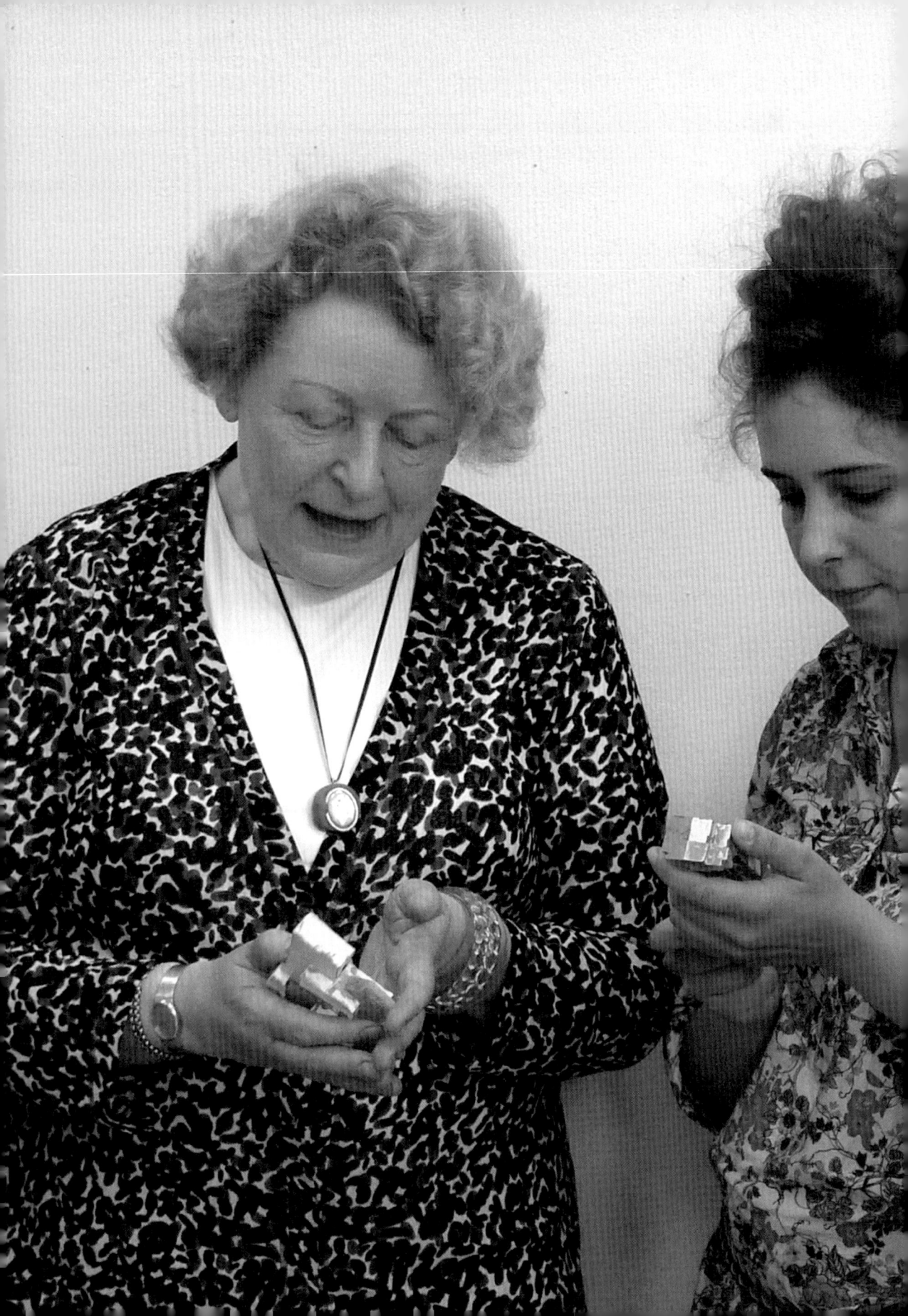

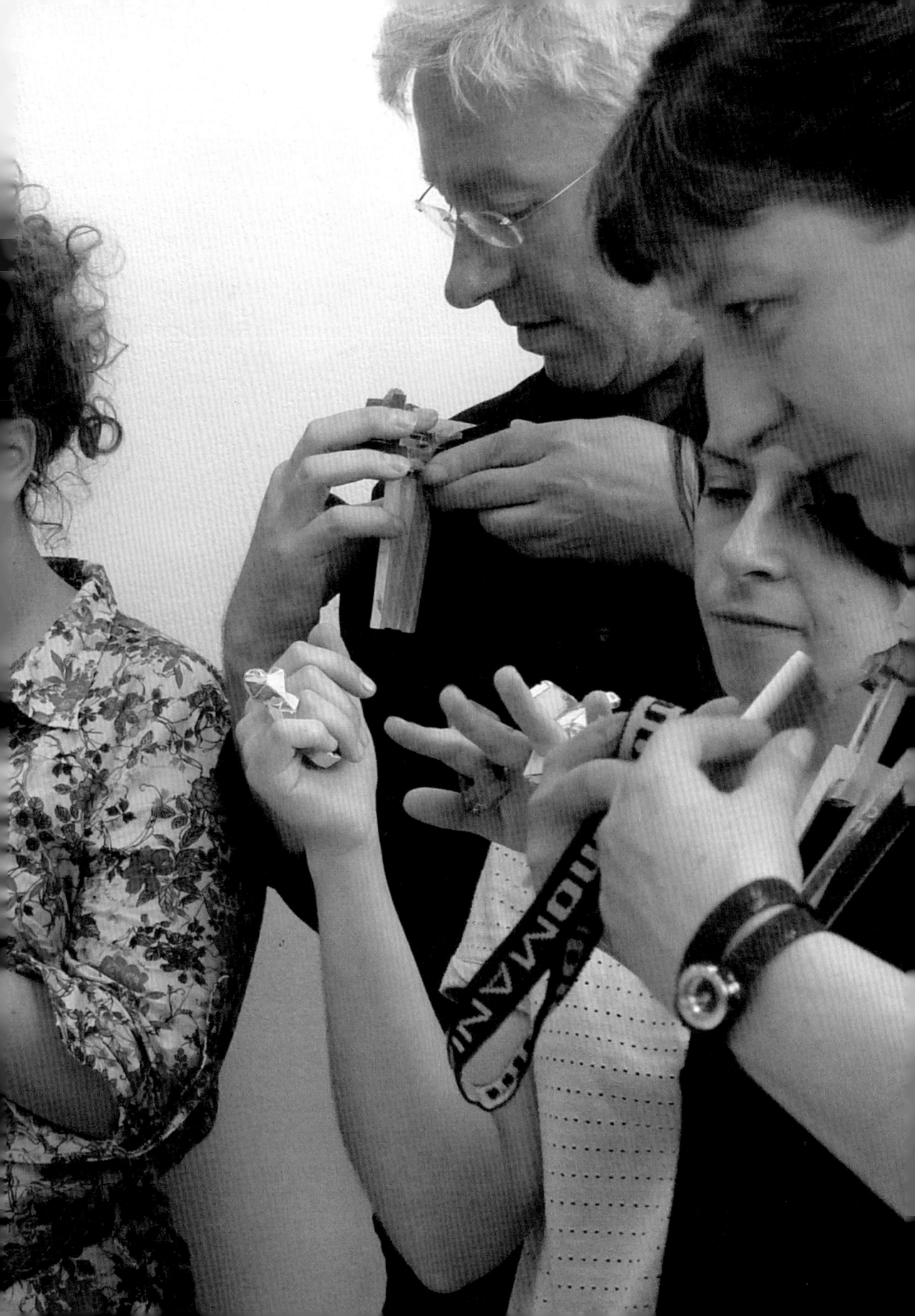